FLUSH

FLUSH

A BIOGRAPHY

BY

Virginia Woolf, 1882-1941.

HARCOURT, BRACE AND COMPANY

NEW YORK

Contents

Illustrations

I

CHAPTER ONE

Three Mile Cross

IT IS universally admitted that the family from which the subject of this memoir claims descent is one of the greatest antiquity. Therefore it is not strange that the origin of the name itself is lost in obscurity. Many million years ago the country which is now called Spain seethed uneasily in the ferment of creation. Ages passed; vegetation appeared; where there is vegetation the law of Nature has decreed that there shall be rabbits; where there are rabbits, Providence has ordained there shall be dogs. There is nothing in this that calls for question or comment. But when we ask why the dog that caught the rabbit was called a Spaniel, then doubts and difficulties begin. Some historians say that when the Carthaginians landed in Spain the common soldiers shouted with one accord "Span! Span!"—for rabbits darted from every scrub, from every bush. The land was alive with rabbits. And *Span* in the Carthaginian tongue signifies Rabbit. Thus the land was called

Hispania, or Rabbit-land, and the dogs, which were almost instantly perceived in full pursuit of the rabbits, were called Spaniels or rabbit dogs.

There many of us would be content to let the matter rest; but truth compels us to add that there is another school of thought which thinks differently. The word Hispania, these scholars say, has nothing whatever to do with the Carthaginian word *span*. Hispania derives from the Basque word *españa*, signifying an edge or boundary. If that is so, rabbits, bushes, dogs, soldiers—the whole of that romantic and pleasant picture, must be dismissed from the mind; and we must simply suppose that the Spaniel is called a spaniel because Spain is called España. As for the third school of antiquaries which maintains that just as a lover calls his mistress monster or monkey, so the Spaniards called their favourite dogs crooked or cragged (the word *españa* can be made to take these meanings) because a spaniel is notoriously the opposite—that is too fanciful a conjecture to be seriously entertained.

Passing over these theories, and many more which need not detain us here, we reach Wales in the middle of the tenth century. The spaniel is already there, brought, some say, by the Spanish clan of

Ebhor or Ivor many centuries previously; and certainly by the middle of the tenth century a dog of high repute and value. "The Spaniel of the King is a pound in value," Howel Dda laid down in his Book of Laws. And when we remember what the pound could buy in the year A.D. 948—how many wives, slaves, horses, oxen, turkeys and geese—it is plain that the spaniel was already a dog of value and reputation. He had his place already by the King's side. His family was held in honour before those of many famous monarchs. He was taking his ease in palaces when the Plantagenets and the Tudors and the Stuarts were following other people's ploughs through other people's mud. Long before the Howards, the Cavendishes or the Russells had risen above the common ruck of Smiths, Joneses and Tomkins, the Spaniel family was a family distinguished and apart. And as the centuries took their way, minor branches broke off from the parent stem. By degrees, as English history pursues its course, there came into existence at least seven famous Spaniel families— the Clumber, the Sussex, the Norfolk, the Black Field, the Cocker, the Irish Water and the English Water, all deriving from the original spaniel of prehistoric days but showing distinct characteristics,

13

and therefore no doubt claiming privileges as distinct. That there was an aristocracy of dogs by the time Queen Elizabeth was on the throne Sir Philip Sidney bears witness: ". . . greyhounds, Spaniels and Hounds," he observes, "whereof the first might seem the Lords, the second the Gentlemen, and the last the Yeomen of dogs," he writes in the *Arcadia*.

But if we are thus led to assume that the Spaniels followed human example, and looked up to Greyhounds as their superiors and considered Hounds beneath them, we have to admit that their aristocracy was founded on better reasons than ours. Such at least must be the conclusion of anyone who studies the laws of the Spaniel Club. By that august body it is plainly laid down what constitute the vices of a spaniel, and what constitute its virtues. Light eyes, for example, are undesirable; curled ears are still worse; to be born with a light nose or a topknot is nothing less than fatal. The merits of the spaniel are equally clearly defined. His head must be smooth, rising without a too-decided stoop from the muzzle; the skull must be comparatively rounded and well developed with plenty of room for brain power; the eyes must be full but not gozzled; the general expression must be one of intelligence and

14

gentleness. The spaniel that exhibits these points is encouraged and bred from; the spaniel who persists in perpetuating topknots and light noses is cut off from the privileges and emoluments of his kind. Thus the judges lay down the law and, laying down the law, impose penalties and privileges which ensure that the law shall be obeyed.

But, if we now turn to human society, what chaos and confusion meet the eye! No Club has any such jurisdiction upon the breed of man. The Heralds College is the nearest approach we have to the Spaniel Club. It at least makes some attempt to preserve the purity of the human family. But when we ask what constitutes noble birth—should our eyes be light or dark, our ears curled or straight, are topknots fatal, our judges merely refer us to our coats of arms. You have none perhaps. Then you are nobody. But once make good your claim to sixteen quarterings, prove your right to a coronet, and then you are not only born they say, but nobly born into the bargain. Hence it is that not a muffineer in all Mayfair lacks its lion couchant or its mermaid rampant. Even our linendrapers mount the Royal Arms above their doors, as though that were proof that their sheets are safe to sleep in. Everywhere rank is

claimed and its virtues are asserted. Yet when we
come to survey the Royal Houses of Bourbon, Haps-
burg and Hohenzollern, decorated with how many
coronets and quarterings, couchant and rampant
with how many lions and leopards, and find them
now in exile, deposed from authority, judged un-
worthy of respect, we can but shake our heads and
admit that the Judges of the Spaniel Club judged
better. Such is the lesson that is enforced directly we
turn from these high matters to consider the early
life of Flush in the family of the Mitfords.

About the end of the eighteenth century a family
of the famous spaniel breed was living near Reading in the house of a certain Dr. Midford or Mitford. That gentleman, in conformity with the canons
of the Heralds College, chose to spell his name with
a *t*, and thus claimed descent from the Northumber-
land family of the Mitfords of Bertram Castle. His
wife was a Miss Russell, and sprang, if remotely,
still decidedly from the ducal house of Bedford. But
the mating of Dr. Mitford's ancestors had been carried on with such wanton disregard for principles
that no bench of judges could have admitted his
claim to be well bred or have allowed him to per-
petuate his kind. His eyes were light; his ears were

curled; his head exhibited the fatal topknot. In other words, he was utterly selfish, recklessly extravagant, worldly, insincere and addicted to gambling. He wasted his own fortune, his wife's fortune, and his daughter's earnings. He deserted them in his prosperity and sponged upon them in his infirmity. Two points he had in his favour indeed, great personal beauty—he was like an Apollo until gluttony and intemperance changed Apollo into Bacchus— and he was genuinely devoted to dogs. But there can be no doubt that, had there been a Man Club corresponding to the Spaniel Club in existence, no spelling of Mitford with a *t* instead of with a *d*, no claim to kinship with the Mitfords of Bertram Castle, would have availed to protect him from contumely and contempt, from all the penalties of outlawry and ostracism, from being branded as a mongrel man unfitted to carry on his kind. But he was a human being. Nothing therefore prevented him from marrying a lady of birth and breeding, from living for over eighty years, from having in his possession several generations of greyhounds and spaniels and from begetting a daughter.

All researches have failed to fix with any certainty the exact year of Flush's birth, let alone the month or the day; but it is likely that he was born some time early in the year 1842. It is also probable that he was directly descended from Tray (*c.* 1816), whose points, preserved unfortunately only in the untrustworthy medium of poetry, prove him to have been a red cocker spaniel of merit. There is every reason to think that Flush was the son of that "real old cocking spaniel" for whom Dr. Mitford refused twenty guineas "on account of his excellence in the field." It is to poetry, alas, that we have to trust for our most detailed description of Flush himself as a young dog. He was of that particular shade of dark brown which in sunshine flashes "all over into gold." His eyes were "startled eyes of hazel bland." His ears were "tasselled"; his "slender feet" were "canopied in fringes" and his tail was broad. Making allowance for the exigencies of rhyme and the inaccuracies of poetic diction, there is nothing here but what would meet with the approval of the Spaniel Club. We cannot doubt that Flush was a pure-bred Cocker of the red variety marked by all the characteristic excellences of his kind.

The first months of his life were passed at Three Mile Cross, a working man's cottage near Reading. Since the Mitfords had fallen on evil days—Kerenhappock was the only servant—the chair-covers were made by Miss Mitford herself and of the cheapest material; the most important article of furniture seems to have been a large table; the most important room a large greenhouse—it is unlikely that Flush was surrounded by any of those luxuries, rain-proof kennels, cement walks, a maid or boy attached to his person, that would now be accorded a dog of his rank. But he throve; he enjoyed with all the vivacity of his temperament most of the pleasures and some of the licences natural to his youth and sex. Miss Mitford, it is true, was much confined to the cottage. She had to read aloud to her father hour after hour; then to play cribbage; then, when at last he slumbered, to write and write and write at the table in the greenhouse in the attempt to pay their bills and settle their debts. But at last the longed-for moment would come. She thrust her papers aside, clapped a hat on her head, took her umbrella and set off for a walk across the fields with her dogs. Spaniels are by nature sympathetic; Flush, as his story proves, had an even excessive appreciation of human emotions. The sight of his dear mistress snuffing the fresh air at last, letting it ruffle her white hair and redden the natural freshness of her face, while the lines on her huge brow smoothed themselves out, excited him to gambols whose wildness was half sympathy with her own delight. As she strode through the long grass, so he leapt hither and thither, parting its green curtain. The cool globes of dew or rain broke in showers of iridescent spray about his nose; the earth, here hard, here soft, here hot, here cold, stung, teased and tickled the soft pads of his feet. Then what a variety of smells interwoven in subtlest combination thrilled his nostrils; strong smells of earth, sweet smells of flowers; nameless smells of leaf and bramble; sour smells as they crossed the road; pungent smells as they entered bean-fields. But suddenly down the wind came tearing a smell sharper, stronger, more lacerating than any—a smell that ripped across his brain stirring a thousand instincts, releasing a million memories—the smell of hare, the smell of fox. Off he flashed like a fish drawn in a rush through water further and further. He forgot his mistress; he forgot all humankind. He heard dark men cry "Span! Span!" He heard whips crack. He raced; he rushed. At last he stopped bewildered; the incantation faded; very slowly, wagging his tail sheepishly, he trotted back across the fields to where Miss Mitford stood shouting "Flush! Flush! Flush!" and waving her umbrella. And once at least the call was even more imperious; the hunting horn roused deeper instincts, summoned wilder and stronger emotions that transcended memory and obliterated grass, trees, hare, rabbit, fox in one wild shout of ecstasy. Love blazed her torch in his eyes; he heard the hunting horn of Venus. Before he was well out of his puppyhood, Flush was a father.

Such conduct in a man even, in the year 1842, would have called for some excuse from a biographer; in a woman no excuse could have availed; her name must have been blotted in ignominy from the page. But the moral code of dogs, whether better or worse, is certainly different from ours, and there was nothing in Flush's conduct in this respect that requires a veil now, or unfitted him for the society of the purest and the chastest in the land then. There is evidence, that is to say, that the elder brother of Dr. Pusey was anxious to buy him. Deducing from the known character of Dr. Pusey the probable character of his brother, there must have been something serious, solid, promising well for future excellence whatever might be the levity of the present in Flush even as a puppy. But a much more significant testi-

21

mony to the attractive nature of his gifts is that, even though Mr. Pusey wished to buy him, Miss Mitford refused to sell him. As she was at her wits' end for money, scarcely knew indeed what tragedy to spin, what annual to edit, and was reduced to the repulsive expedient of asking her friends for help, it must have gone hard with her to refuse the sum offered by the elder brother of Dr. Pusey. Twenty pounds had been offered for Flush's father. Miss Mitford might well have asked ten or fifteen for Flush. Ten or fifteen pounds was a princely sum, a magnificent sum to have at her disposal. With ten or fifteen pounds she might have re-covered her chairs, she might have re-stocked her greenhouse, she might have bought herself an entire wardrobe, and "I have not bought a bonnet, a cloak, a gown, hardly a pair of gloves," she wrote in 1842, "for four years."

But to sell Flush was unthinkable. He was of the rare order of objects that cannot be associated with money. Was he not of the still rarer kind that, because they typify what is spiritual, what is beyond price, become a fitting token of the disinterestedness of friendship; may be offered in that spirit to a friend, if one is so lucky enough as to have one, who is more like a daughter than a friend; to a friend who lies secluded all through the summer months in a back bedroom in Wimpole Street, to a friend who is no other than England's foremost poetess, the brilliant, the doomed, the adored Elizabeth Barrett herself? Such were the thoughts that came more and more frequently to Miss Mitford as she watched Flush rolling and scampering in the sunshine; as she sat by the couch of Miss Barrett in her dark, ivy-shaded London bedroom. Yes; Flush was worthy of Miss Barrett; Miss Barrett was worthy of Flush. The sacrifice was a great one; but the sacrifice must be made. Thus, one day, probably in the early summer of the year 1842, a remarkable couple might have been seen taking their way down Wimpole Street—a very short, stout, shabby, elderly lady, with a bright red face and bright white hair, who led by the chain a very spirited, very inquisitive, very well-bred golden cocker spaniel puppy. They walked almost the whole length of the street until at last they paused at No. 50. Not without trepidation, Miss Mitford rang the bell.

Even now perhaps nobody rings the bell of a house in Wimpole Street without trepidation. It is the most august of London streets, the most imper-

sonal. Indeed, when the world seems tumbling to
ruin, and civilisation rocks on its foundations, one
has only to go to Wimpole Street; to pace that avenue; to survey those houses; to consider their uni-
formity; to marvel at the window curtains and their
consistency; to admire the brass knockers and their
regularity; to observe butchers tendering joints and
cooks receiving them; to reckon the incomes of the
inhabitants and infer their consequent submission
to the laws of God and man—one has only to go
to Wimpole Street and drink deep of the peace
breathed by authority in order to heave a sigh of
thankfulness that, while Corinth has fallen and Mes-
sina has tumbled, while crowns have blown down
the wind and old Empires have gone up in flames,
Wimpole Street has remained unmoved and, turning from Wimpole Street into Oxford Street, a
prayer rises in the heart and bursts from the lips that
not a brick of Wimpole Street may be re-pointed,
not a curtain washed, not a butcher fail to tender or
a cook to receive the sirloin, the haunch, the breast,
the ribs of mutton and beef for ever and ever, for
as long as Wimpole Street remains, civilisation is
secure.

The butlers of Wimpole Street move ponderously

MISS MITFORD

even today; in the summer of 1842 they were more
deliberate still. The laws of livery were then more
stringent; the ritual of the green baize apron for
cleaning silver; of the striped waistcoat and swal-
low-tail black coat for opening the hall door, was
more closely observed. It is likely then that Miss
Mitford and Flush were kept waiting at least three
minutes and a half on the door-step. At last, however, the door of number fifty was flung wide; Miss
Mitford and Flush were ushered in. Miss Mitford
was a frequent visitor; there was nothing to sur-
prise, though something to subdue her, in the sight
of the Barrett family mansion. But the effect upon
Flush must have been overwhelming in the extreme.
Until this moment he had set foot in no house but
the working man's cottage at Three Mile Cross. The
boards there were bare; the mats were frayed; the
chairs were cheap. Here there was nothing bare,
nothing frayed, nothing cheap—that Flush could
see at a glance. Mr. Barrett, the owner, was a rich
merchant; he had a large family of grown-up sons
and daughters, and a retinue, proportionately large,
of servants. His house was furnished in the fashion
of the late thirties, with some tincture, no doubt, of
that Eastern fantasy which had led him when he

25

built a house in Shropshire to adorn it with the domes and crescents of Moorish architecture. Here in Wimpole Street such extravagance would not be allowed; but we may suppose that the high dark rooms were full of ottomans and carved mahogany; tables were twisted; filigree ornaments stood upon them; daggers and swords hung upon wine-dark walls; curious objects brought from his East Indian property stood in recesses, and thick rich carpets clothed the floors.

But as Flush trotted up behind Miss Mitford, who was behind the butler, he was more astonished by what he smelt than by what he saw. Up the funnel of the staircase came warm whiffs of joints roasting, of fowls basting, of soups simmering—ravishing almost as food itself to nostrils used to the meagre savour of Kerenhappock's penurious frys and hashes. Mixing with the smell of food were further smells—smells of cedarwood and sandalwood and mahogany; scents of male bodies and female bodies; of men servants and maid servants; of coats and trousers; of crinolines and mantles; of curtains of tapestry, of curtains of plush; of coal dust and fog; of wine and cigars. Each room as he passed it—dining-room, drawing-room, library, bedroom—wafted out its

own contribution to the general stew; while, as he
set down first one paw and then another, each was
caressed and retained by the sensuality of rich pile
carpets closing amorously over it. At length they
reached a closed door at the back of the house. A
gentle tap was given; gently the door was opened.

Miss Barrett's bedroom—for such it was—must
by all accounts have been dark. The light, normally
obscured by a curtain of green damask, was in summer further dimmed by the ivy, the scarlet runners,
the convolvuluses and the nasturtiums which grew in
the window-box. At first Flush could distinguish
nothing in the pale greenish gloom but five white
globes glimmering mysteriously in mid-air. But
again it was the smell of the room that overpowered
him. Only a scholar who has descended step by step
into a mausoleum and there finds himself in a crypt,
crusted with fungus, slimy with mould, exuding sour
smells of decay and antiquity, while half-obliterated
marble busts gleam in mid-air and all is dimly seen
by the light of the small swinging lamp which he
holds, and dips and turns, glancing now here, now
there—only the sensations of such an explorer into
the buried vaults of a ruined city can compare with
the riot of emotions that flooded Flush's nerves as

27

he stood for the first time in an invalid's bedroom, in Wimpole Street, and smelt eau de cologne.

Very slowly, very dimly, with much sniffing and pawing, Flush by degrees distinguished the outlines of several articles of furniture. That huge object by the window was perhaps a wardrobe. Next to it stood, conceivably, a chest of drawers. In the middle of the room swam up to the surface what seemed to be a table with a ring round it; and then the vague amorphous shapes of armchair and table emerged. But everything was disguised. On top of the wardrobe stood three white busts; the chest of drawers was surmounted by a bookcase; the bookcase was pasted over with crimson merino; the washing-table had a coronal of shelves upon it; on top of the shelves that were on top of the washing-table stood two more busts. Nothing in the room was itself; everything was something else. Even the window-blind was not a simple muslin blind; it was a painted fabric with a design of castles and gateways and groves of trees, and there were several peasants taking a walk. Looking-glasses further distorted these already distorted objects so that there seemed to be ten busts of ten poets instead of five; four tables instead of two. And suddenly there was a more ter-

rifying confusion still. Suddenly Flush saw staring
back at him from a hole in the wall another dog with
bright eyes flashing, and tongue lolling! He paused
amazed. He advanced in awe.

Thus advancing, thus withdrawing, Flush scarcely
heard, save as the distant drone of wind among the
tree-tops, the murmur and patter of voices talking.
He pursued his investigations, cautiously, nervously,
as an explorer in a forest softly advances his foot,
uncertain whether that shadow is a lion, or that root
a cobra. At last, however, he was aware of huge
objects in commotion over him; and, unstrung as he
was by the experiences of the past hour, he hid himself, trembling, behind a screen. The voices ceased.
A door shut. For one instant he paused, bewildered,
unstrung. Then with a pounce as of clawed tigers
memory fell upon him. He felt himself alone—deserted. He rushed to the door. It was shut. He
pawed, he listened. He heard footsteps descending.
He knew them for the familiar footsteps of his mistress. They stopped. But no—on they went, down
they went. Miss Mitford was slowly, was heavily,
was reluctantly descending the stairs. And as she
went, as he heard her footsteps fade, panic seized
upon him. Door after door shut in his face as Miss

Mitford went downstairs; they shut on freedom; on fields; on hares; on grass; on his adored, his venerated mistress—on the dear old woman who had washed him and beaten him and fed him from her own plate when she had none too much to eat herself—on all he had known of happiness and love and human goodness! There! The front door slammed. He was alone. She had deserted him.

Then such a wave of despair and anguish overwhelmed him, the irrevocableness and implacability of fate so smote him, that he lifted up his head and howled aloud. A voice said "Flush." He did not hear it. "Flush," it repeated a second time. He started. He had thought himself alone. He turned. Was there something alive in the room with him? Was there something on the sofa? In the wild hope that this being, whatever it was, might open the door, that he might still rush after Miss Mitford and find her—that this was some game of hide-and-seek such as they used to play in the greenhouse at home—Flush darted to the sofa.

"Oh, Flush!" said Miss Barrett. For the first time she looked him in the face. For the first time Flush looked at the lady lying on the sofa.

Each was surprised. Heavy curls hung down on

either side of Miss Barrett's face; large bright eyes
shone out; a large mouth smiled. Heavy ears hung
down on either side of Flush's face; his eyes, too,
were large and bright: his mouth was wide. There
was a likeness between them. As they gazed at each
other each felt: Here am I—and then each felt: But
how different! Hers was the pale worn face of an
invalid, cut off from air, light, freedom. His was the
warm ruddy face of a young animal; instinct with
health and energy. Broken asunder, yet made in the
same mould, could it be that each completed what
was dormant in the other? She might have been—all
that; and he— But no. Between them lay the widest
gulf that can separate one being from another. She
spoke. He was dumb. She was woman; he was dog.
Thus closely united, thus immensely divided, they
gazed at each other. Then with one bound Flush
sprang on to the sofa and laid himself where he was
to lie for ever after—on the rug at Miss Barrett's
feet.

2

CHAPTER TWO

The Back Bedroom

THE summer of 1842 was, historians tell us, not much different from other summers, yet to Flush it was so different that he must have doubted if the world itself were the same. It was a summer spent in a bedroom; a summer spent with Miss Barrett. It was a summer spent in London, spent in the heart of civilisation. At first he saw nothing but the bedroom and its furniture, but that alone was surprising enough. To identify, distinguish and call by their right names all the different articles he saw there was confusing enough. And he had scarcely accustomed himself to the tables, to the busts, to the washing-stands—the smell of eau de cologne still lacerated his nostrils, when there came one of those rare days which are fine but not windy, warm but not baking, dry but not dusty, when an invalid can take the air. The day came when Miss Barrett could safely risk the huge adventure of going shopping with her sister.

The carriage was ordered; Miss Barrett rose from
her sofa; veiled and muffled, she descended the stairs.
Flush of course went with her. He leapt into the carriage by her side. Couched on her lap, the whole
pomp of London at its most splendid burst on his
astonished eyes. They drove along Oxford Street.
He saw houses made almost entirely of glass. He
saw windows laced across with glittering streamers;
heaped with gleaming mounds of pink, purple, yellow, rose. The carriage stopped. He entered mysterious arcades filmed with clouds and webs of tinted
gauze. A million airs from China, from Arabia,
wafted their frail incense into the remotest fibres of
his senses. Swiftly over the counters flashed yards of
gleaming silk; more darkly, more slowly rolled the
ponderous bombazine. Scissors snipped; coins sparkled. Paper was folded; string tied. What with nod-
ding plumes, waving streamers, tossing horses, yellow liveries, passing faces, leaping, dancing up,
down, Flush, satiated with the multiplicity of his
sensations, slept, drowsed, dreamt and knew no more
until he was lifted out of the carriage and the door
of Wimpole Street shut on him again.

And next day, as the fine weather continued, Miss
Barrett ventured upon an even more daring exploit

—she had herself drawn up Wimpole Street in a bath-chair. Again Flush went with her. For the first time he heard his nails click upon the hard paving-stones of London. For the first time the whole battery of a London street on a hot summer's day assaulted his nostrils. He smelt the swooning smells that lie in the gutters; the bitter smells that corrode iron railings; the fuming, heady smells that rise from basements—smells more complex, corrupt, violently contrasted and compounded than any he had smelt in the fields near Reading; smells that lay far beyond the range of the human nose; so that while the chair went on, he stopped, amazed; smelling, savouring, until a jerk at his collar dragged him on. And also, as he trotted up Wimpole Street behind Miss Barrett's chair he was dazed by the passage of human bodies. Petticoats swished at his head; trousers brushed his flanks; sometimes a wheel whizzed an inch from his nose; the wind of destruction roared in his ears and fanned the feathers of his paws as a van passed. Then he plunged in terror. Mercifully the chain tugged at his collar; Miss Barrett held him tight, or he would have rushed to destruction.

At last, with every nerve throbbing and every

sense singing, he reached Regent's Park. And then when he saw once more, after years of absence it seemed, grass, flowers and trees, the old hunting cry of the fields hallooed in his ears and he dashed forward to run as he had run in the fields at home. But now a heavy weight jerked at his throat; he was thrown back on his haunches. Were there not trees and grass? he asked. Were these not the signals of freedom? Had he not always leapt forward directly Miss Mitford started on her walk? Why was he a prisoner here? He paused. Here, he observed, the flowers were massed far more thickly than at home; they stood, plant by plant, rigidly in narrow plots. The plots were intersected by hard black paths. Men in shiny top-hats marched ominously up and down the paths. At the sight of them he shuddered closer to the chair. He gladly accepted the protection of the chain. Thus before many of these walks were over a new conception had entered his brain. Setting one thing beside another, he had arrived at a conclusion. Where there are flower-beds there are asphalt paths; where there are flower-beds and asphalt paths, there are men in shiny top-hats; where there are flower-beds and asphalt paths and men in shiny top-hats, dogs must be led on chains. Without

being able to decipher a word of the placard at the
Gate, he had learnt his lesson—in Regent's Park
dogs must be led on chains.

And to this nucleus of knowledge, born from the
strange experiences of the summer of 1842, soon ad-
hered another: dogs are not equal, but different.
At Three Mile Cross Flush had mixed impartially
with tap-room dogs and the Squire's greyhounds;
he had known no difference between the tinker's
dog and himself. Indeed it is probable that the
mother of his child, though by courtesy called Spaniel, was nothing but a mongrel, eared in one way,
tailed in another. But the dogs of London, Flush
soon discovered, are strictly divided into different
classes. Some are chained dogs; some run wild. Some
take their airings in carriages and drink from purple
jars; others are unkempt and uncollared and pick up
a living in the gutter. Dogs therefore, Flush began
to suspect, differ; some are high, others low; and his
suspicions were confirmed by snatches of talk held
in passing with the dogs of Wimpole Street. "See
that scallywag? A mere mongrel! . . . By gad,
that's a fine Spaniel. One of the best blood in Brit-
ain! . . . Pity his ears aren't a shade more curly.
. . . There's a topknot for you!"

39

From such phrases, from the accent of praise or derision in which they were spoken, at the pillar-box or outside the public-house where the footmen were exchanging racing tips, Flush knew before the summer had passed that there is no equality among dogs: there are high dogs and low dogs. Which, then, was he? No sooner had Flush got home than he examined himself carefully in the looking-glass. Heaven be praised, he was a dog of birth and breeding! His head was smooth; his eyes were prominent but not gozzled; his feet were feathered; he was the equal of the best-bred cocker in Wimpole Street. He noted with approval the purple jar from which he drank— such are the privileges of rank; he bent his head quietly to have the chain fixed to his collar—such are its penalties. When about this time Miss Barrett observed him staring in the glass, she was mistaken. He was a philosopher, she thought, meditating the difference between appearance and reality. On the contrary, he was an aristocrat considering his points.

But the fine summer days were soon over; the autumn winds began to blow; and Miss Barrett settled down to a life of complete seclusion in her bedroom. Flush's life was also changed. His outdoor education was supplemented by that of the bedroom, and this, to a dog of Flush's temperament, was the most drastic that could have been invented. His only airings, and these were brief and perfunctory, were taken in the company of Wilson, Miss Barrett's maid. For the rest of the day he kept his station on the sofa at Miss Barrett's feet. All his natural instincts were thwarted and contradicted. When the autumn winds had blown last year in Berkshire he had run in wild scampering across the stubble; now at the sound of the ivy tapping on the pane Miss Barrett asked Wilson to see to the fastenings of the window. When the leaves of the scarlet runners and nasturtiums in the window-box yellowed and fell she drew her Indian shawl more closely round her. When the October rain lashed the window Wilson lit the fire and heaped up the coals. Autumn deepened into winter and the first fogs jaundiced the air. Wilson and Flush could scarcely grope their way to the pillar-box or to the chemist. When they came back, nothing could be seen in the room but the pale busts glimmering wanly on the tops of the wardrobes; the peasants and the castle had vanished on the blind; blank yellow filled the pane. Flush felt that he and Miss Barrett lived alone together in a cushioned and firelit cave. The traffic droned on perpetually outside with muffled reverberations; now and again a voice went calling hoarsely, "Old chairs and baskets to mend," down the street: sometimes there was a jangle of organ music, coming nearer and louder; going further and fading away. But none of these sounds meant freedom, or action, or exercise. The wind and the rain, the wild days of autumn and the cold days of mid-winter, all alike meant nothing to Flush except warmth and stillness; the lighting of lamps, the drawing of curtains and the poking of the fire.

At first the strain was too great to be borne. He could not help dancing round the room on a windy autumn day when the partridges must be scattering over the stubble. He thought he heard guns on the breeze. He could not help running to the door with his hackles raised when a dog barked outside. And yet when Miss Barrett called him back, when she laid her hand on his collar, he could not deny that another feeling, urgent, contradictory, disagreeable —he did not know what to call it or why he obeyed it—restrained him. He lay still at her feet. To resign, to control, to suppress the most violent instincts of his nature—that was the prime lesson of

the bedroom school, and it was one of such portentous difficulty that many scholars have learnt
Greek with less—many battles have been won that
cost their generals not half such pain. But then,
Miss Barrett was the teacher. Between them, Flush
felt more and more strongly, as the weeks wore on,
was a bond, an uncomfortable yet thrilling tight-
ness; so that if his pleasure was her pain, then his
pleasure was pleasure no longer but three parts pain.
The truth of this was proved every day. Somebody
opened the door and whistled him to come. Why
should he not go out? He longed for air and exercise; his limbs were cramped with lying on the sofa.
He had never grown altogether used to the smell of
eau de cologne. But no—though the door stood open,
he would not leave Miss Barrett. He hesitated half-
way to the door and then went back to the sofa.
"Flushie," wrote Miss Barrett, "is my friend—my
companion—and loves me better than he loves the
sunshine without." She could not go out. She was
chained to the sofa. "A bird in a cage would have as
good a story," she wrote, as she had. And Flush, to
whom the whole world was free, chose to forfeit all
the smells of Wimpole Street in order to lie by her
side.

And yet sometimes the tie would almost break; there were vast gaps in their understanding. Sometimes they would lie and stare at each other in blank bewilderment. Why, Miss Barrett wondered, did Flush tremble suddenly, and whimper and start and listen? She could hear nothing; she could see nothing; there was nobody in the room with them. She could not guess that Folly, her sister's little King Charles, had passed the door; or that Catiline, the Cuba bloodhound, had been given a mutton-bone by a footman in the basement. But Flush knew; he heard; he was ravaged by the alternate rages of lust and greed. Then with all her poet's imagination Miss Barrett could not divine what Wilson's wet umbrella meant to Flush; what memories it recalled, of forests and parrots and wild trumpeting elephants; nor did she know, when Mr. Kenyon stumbled over the bell-pull, that Flush heard dark men cursing in the mountains; the cry, "Span! Span!" rang in his ears, and it was in some muffled, ancestral rage that he bit him.

Flush was equally at a loss to account for Miss Barrett's emotions. There she would lie hour after hour passing her hand over a white page with a black stick; and her eyes would suddenly fill with

44

tears; but why? "Ah, my dear Mr. Horne," she was
writing. "And then came the failure in my health
. . . and then the enforced exile to Torquay . . .
which gave a nightmare to my life for ever, and
robbed it of more than I can speak of here; do not
speak of that anywhere. *Do not speak of that,* dear
Mr. Horne." But there was no sound in the room,
no smell to make Miss Barrett cry. Then again Miss
Barrett, still agitating her stick, burst out laughing.
She had drawn "a very neat and characteristic portrait of Flush, humorously made rather like myself,"
and she had written under it that it "only fails of being an excellent substitute for mine through being
more worthy than I can be counted." What was
there to laugh at in the black smudge that she held
out for Flush to look at? He could smell nothing; he
could hear nothing. There was nobody in the room
with them. The fact was that they could not com-
municate with words, and it was a fact that led undoubtedly to much misunderstanding. Yet did it not
lead also to a peculiar intimacy? "Writing,"—Miss
Barrett once exclaimed after a morning's toil, "writing, writing . . ." After all, she may have thought,
do words say everything? Can words say anything?
Do not words destroy the symbol that lies beyond

45

the reach of words? Once at least Miss Barrett seems
to have found it so. She was lying, thinking; she
had forgotten Flush altogether, and her thoughts
were so sad that the tears fell upon the pillow. Then
suddenly a hairy head was pressed against her; large
bright eyes shone in hers; and she started. Was it
Flush, or was it Pan? Was she no longer an invalid
in Wimpole Street, but a Greek nymph in some dim
grove in Arcady? And did the bearded god himself
press his lips to hers? For a moment she was trans-
formed; she was a nymph and Flush was Pan. The
sun burnt and love blazed. But suppose Flush had
been able to speak—would he not have said something sensible about the potato disease in Ireland?

So, too, Flush felt strange stirrings at work within
him. When he saw Miss Barrett's thin hands deli-
cately lifting some silver box or pearl ornament
from the ringed table, his own furry paws seemed
to contract and he longed that they should fine
themselves to ten separate fingers. When he heard
her low voice syllabling innumerable sounds, he
longed for the day when his own rough roar would
issue like hers in the little simple sounds that had
such mysterious meaning. And when he watched the
same fingers for ever crossing a white page with a

straight stick, he longed for the time when he too should blacken paper as she did.

And yet, had he been able to write as she did? —The question is superfluous happily, for truth compels us to say that in the year 1842-43 Miss Barrett was not a nymph but an invalid; Flush was not a poet but a red cocker spaniel; and Wimpole Street was not Arcady but Wimpole Street.

So the long hours went by in the back bedroom with nothing to mark them but the sound of steps passing on the stairs; and the distant sound of the front door shutting, and the sound of a broom tapping, and the sound of the postman knocking. In the room coals clicked; the lights and shadows shifted themselves over the brows of the five pale busts, over the bookcase and its red merino. But sometimes the step on the stair did not pass the door; it stopped outside. The handle was seen to spin round; the door actually opened; somebody came in. Then how strangely the furniture changed its look! What extraordinary eddies of sound and smell were at once set in circulation! How they washed round the legs of tables and impinged on the sharp edges of the wardrobe! Probably it was Wilson, with a tray of food or a glass of medicine; or it might be one of

Miss Barrett's two sisters—Arabel or Henrietta; or
it might be one of Miss Barrett's seven brothers—
Charles, Samuel, George, Henry, Alfred, Septimus
or Octavius. But once or twice a week Flush was
aware that something more important was about to
happen. The bed would be carefully disguised as a
sofa. The armchair would be drawn up beside it;
Miss Barrett herself would be wrapped becomingly
in Indian shawls; the toilet things would be scru-
pulously hidden under the busts of Chaucer and
Homer; Flush himself would be combed and
brushed. At about two or three in the afternoon
there was a peculiar, distinct and different tap at
the door. Miss Barrett flushed, smiled and stretched
out her hand. Then in would come—perhaps dear
Miss Mitford, rosy and shiny and chattering, with a
bunch of geraniums. Or it might be Mr. Kenyon, a
stout, well-groomed elderly gentleman, radiating
benevolence, provided with a book. Or it might be
Mrs. Jameson, a lady who was the very opposite of
Mr. Kenyon to look at—a lady with "a very light
complexion—pale, lucid, eyes; thin colourless lips
. . . a nose and chin projective without breadth."
Each had his or her own manner, smell, tone and accent. Miss Mitford burbled and chattered, was fly-

away yet substantial; Mr. Kenyon was urbane and cultured and mumbled slightly because he had lost two front teeth; Mrs. Jameson had lost none of her teeth, and moved as sharply and precisely as she spoke.

Lying couched at Miss Barrett's feet, Flush let the voices ripple over him, hour by hour. On and on they went. Miss Barrett laughed, expostulated, exclaimed, sighed too, and laughed again. At last, greatly to Flush's relief, little silences came—even in the flow of Miss Mitford's conversation. Could it be seven already? She had been there since midday! She must really run to catch her train. Mr. Kenyon shut his book—he had been reading aloud—and stood with his back to the fire; Mrs. Jameson with a sharp, angular movement pressed each finger of her glove sharp down. And Flush was patted by this one and had his ear pulled by another. The routine of leave-taking was intolerably prolonged; but at last Mrs. Jameson, Mr. Kenyon, and even Miss Mitford had risen, had said good-bye, had remembered something, had lost something, had found something, had reached the door, had opened it, and were—Heaven be praised—gone at last.

Miss Barrett sank back very white, very tired on

her pillows. Flush crept closer to her. Mercifully
they were alone again. But the visitor had stayed so
long that it was almost dinner-time. Smells began
to rise from the basement. Wilson was at the door
with Miss Barrett's dinner on a tray. It was set down
on the table beside her and the covers lifted. But
what with the dressing and the talking, what with
the heat of the room and the agitation of the fare-
wells, Miss Barrett was too tired to eat. She gave a
little sigh when she saw the plump mutton chop, or
the wing of partridge or chicken that had been sent
up for her dinner. So long as Wilson was in the
room she fiddled about with her knife and fork. But
directly the door was shut and they were alone, she
made a sign. She held up her fork. A whole chicken's
wing was impaled upon it. Flush advanced. Miss
Barrett nodded. Very gently, very cleverly, without
spilling a crumb, Flush removed the wing; swallowed it down and left no trace behind. Half a rice
pudding clotted with thick cream went the same
way. Nothing could have been neater, more effec-
tive than Flush's co-operation. He was lying couched
as usual at Miss Barrett's feet, apparently asleep,
Miss Barrett was lying rested and restored, apparently having made an excellent dinner, when once

more a step that was heavier, more deliberate and firmer than any other, stopped on the stair; solemnly a knock sounded that was no tap of enquiry but a demand for admittance; the door opened and in came the blackest, the most formidable of elderly men—Mr. Barrett himself. His eye at once sought the tray. Had the meal been eaten? Had his commands been obeyed? Yes, the plates were empty. Signifying his approval of his daughter's obedience, Mr. Barrett lowered himself heavily into the chair by her side. As that dark body approached him, shivers of terror and horror ran down Flush's spine. So a savage couched in flowers shudders when the thunder growls and he hears the voice of God. Then Wilson whistled; and Flush, slinking guiltily, as if Mr. Barrett could read his thoughts and those thoughts were evil, crept out of the room and rushed downstairs. A force had entered the bedroom which he dreaded; a force that he was powerless to withstand. Once he burst in unexpectedly. Mr. Barrett was on his knees praying by his daughter's side.

3

The Hooded Man

SUCH an education as this, in the back bedroom at
Wimpole Street, would have told upon an ordinary
dog. And Flush was not an ordinary dog. He was
high-spirited, yet reflective; canine, but highly sensitive to human emotions also. Upon such a dog the
atmosphere of the bedroom told with peculiar force.
We cannot blame him if his sensibility was culti-
vated rather to the detriment of his sterner qualities.
Naturally, lying with his head pillowed on a Greek
lexicon, he came to dislike barking and biting; he
came to prefer the silence of the cat to the robust-
ness of the dog; and human sympathy to either.
Miss Barrett, too, did her best to refine and educate
his powers still further. Once she took a harp from
the window and asked him, as she laid it by his side,
whether he thought that the harp, which made music,
was itself alive? He looked and listened; pondered,
it seemed, for a moment in doubt and then decided
that it was not. Then she would make him stand

with her in front of the looking-glass and ask him why he barked and trembled. Was not the little brown dog opposite himself? But what is "oneself"? Is it the thing people see? Or is it the thing one is? So Flush pondered that question too, and, unable to solve the problem of reality, pressed closer to Miss Barrett and kissed her "expressively." *That* was real at any rate.

Fresh from such problems, with such emotional dilemmas agitating his nervous system, he went downstairs, and we cannot be surprised if there was something—a touch of the supercilious, of the superior—in his bearing that roused the rage of Catiline, the savage Cuba bloodhound, so that he set upon him and bit him and sent him howling upstairs to Miss Barrett for sympathy. Flush "is no hero," she concluded; but why was he no hero? Was it not partly on her account? She was too just not to realize that it was for her that he had sacrificed his courage, as it was for her that he had sacrificed the sun and the air. This nervous sensibility had its drawbacks, no doubt—she was full of apologies when he flew at Mr. Kenyon and bit him for stumbling over the bell-pull; it was annoying when he moaned piteously all night because he was not allowed to sleep on her bed—when he refused to eat unless she fed him; but she took the blame and bore the inconvenience because, after all, Flush loved her. He had refused the air and the sun for her sake. "He is worth loving, is he not?" she asked of Mr. Horne. And whatever answer Mr. Horne might give, Miss Barrett was positive of her own. She loved Flush, and Flush was worthy of her love.

It seemed as if nothing were to break that tie— as if the years were merely to compact and cement it; and as if those years were to be all the years of their natural lives. Eighteen-forty-two turned into eighteen-forty-three; eighteen-forty-three into eighteen-forty-four; eighteen-forty-four into eighteen-forty-five. Flush was no longer a puppy; he was a dog of four or five; he was a dog in the full prime of life—and still Miss Barrett lay on her sofa in Wimpole Street and still Flush lay on the sofa at her feet. Miss Barrett's life was the life of "a bird in its cage." She sometimes kept the house for weeks at a time, and when she left it, it was only for an hour or two, to drive to a shop in a carriage, or to be wheeled to Regent's Park in a bath-chair. The Barretts never left London. Mr. Barrett, the seven brothers, the two sisters, the butler, Wilson and

the maids, Catiline, Folly, Miss Barrett and Flush
all went on living at 50 Wimpole Street, eating in
the dining-room, sleeping in the bedrooms, smoking
in the study, cooking in the kitchen, carrying hot-
water cans and emptying the slops from January to
December. The chair-covers became slightly soiled;
the carpets slightly worn; coal dust, mud, soot, fog,
vapours of cigar smoke and wine and meat accumulated in crevices, in cracks, in fabrics, on the tops of
picture-frames, in the scrolls of carvings. And the
ivy that hung over Miss Barrett's bedroom window
flourished; its green curtain became thicker and
thicker, and in summer the nasturtiums and the scarlet runners rioted together in the window-box.

But one night early in January 1845 the postman
knocked. Letters fell into the box as usual. Wilson
went downstairs to fetch the letters as usual. Everything was as usual—every night the postman
knocked, every night Wilson fetched the letters,
every night there was a letter for Miss Barrett. But
tonight the letter was not the same letter; it was a
different letter. Flush saw that, even before the envelope was broken. He knew it from the way that
Miss Barrett took it; turned it; looked at the vigorous, jagged writing of her name. He knew it from

the indescribable tremor in her fingers, from the impetuosity with which they tore the flap open, from the absorption with which she read. He watched her read. And as she read he heard, as when we are half asleep we hear through the clamour of the street some bell ringing and know that it is addressed to us, alarmingly yet faintly, as if someone far away were trying to rouse us with the warning of fire, or burglary, or some menace against our peace and we start in alarm before we wake—so Flush, as Miss Barrett read the little blotted sheet, heard a bell rousing him from his sleep; warning him of some danger menacing his safety and bidding him sleep no more. Miss Barrett read the letter quickly; she read the letter slowly; she returned it carefully to its envelope. She too slept no more.

Again, a few nights later, there was the same letter on Wilson's tray. Again it was read quickly, read slowly, read over and over again. Then it was put away carefully, not in the drawer with the voluminous sheets of Miss Mitford's letters, but by itself. Now Flush paid the full price of long years of accumulated sensibility lying couched on cushions at Miss Barrett's feet. He could read signs that nobody else could even see. He could tell by the touch of

Miss Barrett's fingers that she was waiting for one thing only—for the postman's knock, for the letter on the tray. She would be stroking him perhaps with a light, regular movement; suddenly—there was the rap—her fingers constricted; he would be held in a vice while Wilson came upstairs. Then she took the letter and he was loosed and forgotten.

Yet, he argued, what was there to be afraid of, so long as there was no change in Miss Barrett's life? And there was no change. No new visitors came. Mr. Kenyon came as usual; Miss Mitford came as usual. The brothers and sisters came; and in the evening Mr. Barrett came. They noticed nothing; they suspected nothing. So he would quieten himself and try to believe, when a few nights passed without the envelope, that the enemy had gone. A man in a cloak, he imagined, a cowled and hooded figure, had passed, like a burglar, rattling the door, and finding it guarded, had slunk away defeated. The danger, Flush tried to make himself believe, was over. The man had gone. And then the letter came again.

As the envelopes came more and more regularly, night after night, Flush began to notice signs of change in Miss Barrett herself. For the first time in

Flush's experience she was irritable and restless. She could not read and she could not write. She stood at the window and looked out. She questioned Wilson anxiously about the weather—was the wind still in the east? Was there any sign of spring in the Park yet? Oh no, Wilson replied; the wind was a cruel east wind still. And Miss Barrett, Flush felt, was at once relieved and annoyed. She coughed. She complained of feeling ill—but not so ill as she usually felt when the wind was in the east. And then, when she was alone, she read over again last night's letter. It was the longest she had yet had. There were many pages, closely covered, darkly blotted, scattered with strange little abrupt hieroglyphics. So much Flush could see, from his station at her feet. But he could make no sense of the words that Miss Barrett was murmuring to herself. Only he could trace her agitation when she came to the end of the page and read aloud (though unintelligibly), "Do you think I shall see you in two months, three months?"

Then she took up her pen and passed it rapidly and nervously over sheet after sheet. But what did they mean—the little words that Miss Barrett wrote? "April is coming. There will be both a May

61

and a June if we live to see such things, and perhaps, after all, we may . . . I will indeed see you when the warm weather has revived me a little. . . . But I shall be afraid of you at first—though I am not, in writing thus. You are Paracelsus, and I am a recluse, with nerves that have been broken on the rack, and now hang loosely, quivering at a step and breath."

Flush could not read what she was writing an inch or two above his head. But he knew just as well as if he could read every word, how strangely his mistress was agitated as she wrote; what contrary desires shook her—that April might come; that April might not come; that she might see this unknown man at once, that she might never see him at all. Flush, too, quivered as she did at a step, at a breath. And remorselessly the days went on. The wind blew out the blind. The sun whitened the busts. A bird sang in the mews. Men went crying fresh flowers to sell down Wimpole Street. All these sounds meant, he knew, that April was coming and May and June—nothing could stop the approach of that dreadful spring. For what was coming with the spring? Some terror—some horror—something that Miss Barrett dreaded, and that Flush dreaded too.

He started now at the sound of a step. But it was only Henrietta. Then there was a knock. It was only Mr. Kenyon. So April passed; and the first twenty days of May. And then, on the 21st of May, Flush knew that the day itself had come. For on Tuesday, the 21st of May, Miss Barrett looked searchingly in the glass; arrayed herself exquisitely in her Indian shawls; bade Wilson draw the armchair close, but not too close; touched this, that and the other; and then sat upright among her pillows. Flush couched himself taut at her feet. They waited, alone together. At last, Marylebone Church clock struck two; they waited. Then Marylebone Church clock struck a single stroke—it was half-past two; and as the single stroke died away, a rap sounded boldly on the front door. Miss Barrett turned pale; she lay very still. Flush lay still too. Upstairs came the dreaded, the inexorable footfall; upstairs, Flush knew, came the cowled and sinister figure of midnight—the hooded man. Now his hand was on the door. The handle spun. There he stood.

"Mr. Browning," said Wilson.

Flush, watching Miss Barrett, saw the colour rush into her face; saw her eyes brighten and her lips open.

"Mr. Browning!" she exclaimed.

Twisting his yellow gloves in his hands, blinking his eyes, well groomed, masterly, abrupt, Mr. Browning strode across the room. He seized Miss Barrett's hand, and sank into the chair by the sofa at her side. Instantly they began to talk.

What was horrible to Flush, as they talked, was his loneliness. Once he had felt that he and Miss Barrett were together, in a firelit cave. Now the cave was no longer firelit; it was dark and damp; Miss Barrett was outside. He looked round him. Everything had changed. The bookcase, the five busts—they were no longer friendly deities presiding approvingly—they were alien, severe. He shifted his position at Miss Barrett's feet. She took no notice. He whined. They did not hear him. At last he lay still in tense and silent agony. The talk went on; but it did not flow and ripple as talk usually flowed and rippled. It leapt and jerked. It stopped and leapt again. Flush had never heard that sound in Miss Barrett's voice before—that vigour, that excitement. Her cheeks were bright as he had never seen them bright; her great eyes blazed as he had never seen them blaze. The clock struck four; and still they talked. Then it struck half-past four. At that Mr. Browning jumped up. A horrid decision, a dreadful boldness marked every movement. In another moment he had wrung Miss Barrett's hand in his; he had taken his hat and gloves; he had said good-bye. They heard him running down the stairs. Smartly the door banged behind him. He was gone.

But Miss Barrett did not sink back in her pillows as she sank back when Mr. Kenyon or Miss Mitford left her. Now she still sat upright; her eyes still burnt; her cheeks still glowed; she seemed still to feel that Mr. Browning was with her. Flush touched her. She recalled him with a start. She patted him lightly, joyfully, on the head. And smiling, she gave him the oddest look—as if she wished that he could talk—as if she expected him too to feel what she felt. And then she laughed, pityingly; as if it were absurd—Flush, poor Flush could feel nothing of what she felt. He could know nothing of what she knew. Never had such wastes of dismal distance separated them. He lay there ignored; he might not have been there, he felt. She no longer remembered his existence.

And that night she ate her chicken to the bone. Not a scrap of potato or of skin was thrown to Flush. When Mr. Barrett came as usual, Flush mar-

velled at his obtuseness. He sat himself down in the
very chair that the man had sat in. His head pressed
the same cushions that the man's had pressed, and
yet he noticed nothing. "Don't you know," Flush
marvelled, "who's been sitting in that chair? Can't
you smell him?" For to Flush the whole room still
reeked of Mr. Browning's presence. The air dashed
past the bookcase, and eddied and curled round the
heads of the five pale busts. But the heavy man sat
by his daughter in entire self-absorption. He noticed
nothing. He suspected nothing. Aghast at his obtuseness, Flush slipped past him out of the room.

But in spite of their astonishing blindness, even
Miss Barrett's family began to notice, as the weeks
passed, a change in Miss Barrett. She left her room
and went down to sit in the drawing-room. Then
she did what she had not done for many a long day
—she actually walked on her own feet as far as
the gate at Devonshire Place with her sister. Her
friends, her family, were amazed at her improve-
ment. But only Flush knew where her strength
came from—it came from the dark man in the armchair. He came again and again and again. First
it was once a week; then it was twice a week. He
came always in the afternoon and left in the after-

noon. Miss Barrett always saw him alone. And on
the days when he did not come, his letters came.
And when he himself was gone, his flowers were
there. And in the mornings when she was alone,
Miss Barrett wrote to him. That dark, taut, abrupt,
vigorous man, with his black hair, his red cheeks
and his yellow gloves, was everywhere. Naturally,
Miss Barrett was better; of course she could walk.
Flush himself felt that it was impossible to lie still.
Old longings revived; a new restlessness possessed
him. Even his sleep was full of dreams. He dreamt
as he had not dreamt since the old days at Three
Mile Cross—of hares starting from the long grass;
of pheasants rocketing up with long tails streaming,
of partridges rising with a whirr from the stubble.
He dreamt that he was hunting, that he was chasing some spotted spaniel, who fled, who escaped
him. He was in Spain; he was in Wales; he was
in Berkshire; he was flying before park-keepers'
truncheons in Regent's Park. Then he opened his
eyes. There were no hares, and no partridges; no
whips cracking and no black men crying "Span!
Span!" There was only Mr. Browning in the armchair talking to Miss Barrett on the sofa.

Sleep became impossible while that man was

there. Flush lay with his eyes wide open, listening. Though he could make no sense of the little words that hurtled over his head from two-thirty to four-thirty sometimes three times a week, he could detect with terrible accuracy that the tone of the words was changing. Miss Barrett's voice had been forced and unnaturally lively at first. Now it had gained a warmth and an ease that he had never heard in it before. And every time the man came, some new sound came into their voices—now they made a grotesque chattering; now they skimmed over him like birds flying widely; now they cooed and clucked, as if they were two birds settled in a nest; and then Miss Barrett's voice, rising again, went soaring and circling in the air; and then Mr. Browning's voice barked out its sharp, harsh clapper of laughter; and then there was only a murmur, a quiet humming sound as the two voices joined together. But as the summer turned to autumn Flush noted, with horrid apprehension, another note. There was a new urgency, a new pressure and energy in the man's voice, at which Miss Barrett, Flush felt, took fright. Her voice fluttered; hesitated; seemed to falter and fade and plead and gasp, as if she were begging for a rest,

68

for a pause, as if she were afraid. Then the man was silent.

Of him they took but little notice. He might have been a log of wood lying there at Miss Barrett's feet for all the attention Mr. Browning paid him. Sometimes he scrubbed his head in a brisk, spasmodic way, energetically, without sentiment, as he passed him. Whatever that scrub might mean, Flush felt nothing but an intense dislike for Mr. Browning. The very sight of him, so well tailored, so tight, so muscular, screwing his yellow gloves in his hand, set his teeth on edge. Oh! to let them meet sharply, completely in the stuff of his trousers! And yet he dared not. Taking it all in all, that winter—1845-6—was the most distressing that Flush had ever known.

The winter passed; and spring came round again. Flush could see no end to the affair; and yet just as a river, though it reflects still trees and grazing cows and rooks returning to the tree-tops, moves inevitably to a waterfall, so those days, Flush knew, were moving to catastrophe. Rumours of change hovered in the air. Sometimes he thought that some vast exodus impended. There was that indefinable stir in the house which precedes—could it be possible?—a journey. Boxes were actually dusted, were,

incredible as it might seem, opened. Then they were
shut again. No, it was not the family that was going to move. The brothers and sisters still went in
and out as usual. Mr. Barrett paid his nightly visit,
after the man had gone, at his accustomed hour.
What was it, then, that was going to happen? for as
the summer of 1846 wore on, Flush was positive
that a change was coming. He could hear it again in
the altered sound of the eternal voices. Miss Barrett's voice, that had been pleading and afraid, lost
its faltering note. It rang out with a determination
and a boldness that Flush had never heard in it before. If only Mr. Barrett could hear the tone in
which she welcomed this usurper, the laugh with
which she greeted him, the exclamation with which
he took her hand in his! But nobody was in the room
with them except Flush. To him the change was of
the most galling nature. It was not merely that Miss
Barrett was changing towards Mr. Browning—she
was changing in every relation—in her feeling towards Flush himself. She treated his advances more
brusquely; she cut short his endearments laugh-
ingly; she made him feel that there was something
petty, silly, affected, in his old affectionate ways.
His vanity was exacerbated. His jealousy was in-

flamed. At last, when July came, he determined to make one violent attempt to regain her favour, and perhaps to oust the newcomer. How to accomplish this double purpose he did not know, and could not plan. But suddenly on the 8th of July his feelings overcame him. He flung himself on Mr. Browning and bit him savagely. At last his teeth met in the immaculate cloth of Mr. Browning's trousers! But the limb inside was hard as iron—Mr. Kenyon's leg had been butter in comparison. Mr. Browning brushed him off with a flick of his hand and went on talking. Neither he nor Miss Barrett seemed to think the attack worthy of attention. Completely foiled, worsted, without a shaft left in his sheath, Flush sank back on his cushions panting with rage and disappointment. But he had misjudged Miss Barrett's insight. When Mr. Browning was gone, she called him to her and inflicted upon him the worst punishment he had ever known. First she slapped his ears—that was nothing; oddly enough the slap was rather to his liking; he would have welcomed another. But then she said in her sober, certain tones that she would never love him again. That shaft went to his heart. All these years they had lived together, shared everything together, and now, for one

moment's failure, she would never love him again.
Then, as if to make her dismissal complete, she took
the flowers that Mr. Browning had brought her and
began to put them in water in a vase. It was an act,
Flush thought, of calculated and deliberate malice;
an act designed to make him feel his own insignifi-
cance completely. "This rose is from him," she
seemed to say, "and this carnation. Let the red shine
by the yellow; and the yellow by the red. And let the
green leaf lie there—" And, setting one flower with
another, she stood back to gaze at them as if he were
before her—the man in the yellow gloves—a mass of
brilliant flowers. But even so, even as she pressed the
leaves and flowers together, she could not altogether
ignore the fixity with which Flush gazed at her. She
could not deny that "expression of quite despair
on his face." She could not but relent. "At last I
said, 'If you are good, Flush, you may come and
say that you are sorry,' on which he dashed across
the room and, trembling all over, kissed first one
of my hands and then another, and put up his paws
to be shaken, and looked into my face with such be-
seeching eyes that you would certainly have forgiven
him just as I did." That was her account of the matter to Mr. Browning; and he of course replied: "Oh,

poor Flush, do you think I do not love and respect
him for his jealous supervision—his slowness to
know another, having once known you?" It was easy
enough for Mr. Browning to be magnanimous, but
that easy magnanimity was perhaps the sharpest
thorn that pressed into Flush's side.

Another incident a few days later showed how
widely they were separated, who had been so close,
how little Flush could now count on Miss Barrett
for sympathy. After Mr. Browning had gone one
afternoon Miss Barrett decided to drive to Regent's
Park with her sister. As they got out at the Park
gate the door of the four-wheeler shut on Flush's
paw. He "cried piteously" and held it up to Miss
Barrett for sympathy. In other days sympathy in
abundance would have been lavished upon him for
less. But now a detached, a mocking, a critical expression came into her eyes. She laughed at him.
She thought he was shamming: ". . . no sooner
had he touched the grass than he began to run without a thought of it," she wrote. And she commented
sarcastically, "Flush always makes the most of his
misfortunes—he is of the Byronic school—*il se pose
en victime.*" But here Miss Barrett, absorbed in her
own emotions, misjudged him completely. If his paw

had been broken, still he would have bounded. That dash was his answer to her mockery; I have done with you—that was the meaning he flashed at her as he ran. The flowers smelt bitter to him; the grass burnt his paws; the dust filled his nostrils with disillusion. But he raced—he scampered. "Dogs must be led on chains"—there was the usual placard; there were the park-keepers with their top-hats and their truncheons to enforce it. But "must" no longer had any meaning for him. The chain of love was broken. He would run where he liked; chase partridges; chase spaniels; splash into the middle of dahlia beds; break brilliant, glowing red and yellow roses. Let the park-keepers throw their truncheons if they chose. Let them dash his brains out. Let him fall dead, disembowelled, at Miss Barrett's feet. He cared nothing. But naturally nothing of the kind happened. Nobody pursued him; nobody noticed him. The solitary park-keeper was talking to a nursemaid. At last he returned to Miss Barrett and she absentmindedly slipped the chain over his neck, and led him home.

After two such humiliations the spirit of an ordinary dog, the spirit even of an ordinary human being, might well have been broken. But Flush, for all his softness and silkiness, had eyes that blazed; had passions that leapt not merely in bright flame but sunk and smouldered. He resolved to meet his enemy face to face and alone. No third person should interrupt this final conflict. It should be fought out by the principals themselves. On the afternoon of Tuesday, the 21st of July, therefore, he slipped downstairs and waited in the hall. He had not long to wait. Soon he heard the tramp of the familiar footstep in the street; he heard the familiar rap on the door. Mr. Browning was admitted. Vaguely aware of the impending attack and determined to meet it in the most conciliatory of spirits, Mr. Browning had come provided with a parcel of cakes. There was Flush waiting in the hall. Mr. Browning made, evidently, some well-meant attempt to caress him; perhaps he even went so far as to offer him a cake. The gesture was enough. Flush sprang upon his enemy with unparalleled violence. His teeth once more met in Mr. Browning's trousers. But unfortunately in the excitement of the moment he forgot what was most essential—silence. He barked; he flung himself on Mr. Browning, barking loudly. The sound was sufficient to alarm the household. Wilson rushed downstairs. Wilson beat him soundly. Wilson overpow-

75

ered him completely. Wilson led him in ignominy away. Ignominy it was—to have attacked Mr. Browning, to have been beaten by Wilson. Mr. Browning had not lifted a finger. Taking his cakes with him, Mr. Browning proceeded unhurt, unmoved, in perfect composure, upstairs, alone to the bedroom. Flush was led away.

After two and a half hours of miserable confinement with parrots and beetles, ferns and saucepans, in the kitchen, Flush was summoned to Miss Barrett's presence. She was lying on the sofa with her sister Arabella beside her. Conscious of the rightness of his cause, Flush went straight to her. But she refused to look at him. He turned to Arabella. She merely said, "Naughty Flush, go away." Wilson was there—the formidable, the implacable Wilson. It was to her that Miss Barrett turned for information. She had beaten him. Wilson said, "because it was right." And, she added, she had only beaten him with her hand. It was upon her evidence that Flush was convicted. The attack, Miss Barrett assumed, had been unprovoked; she credited Mr. Browning with all virtue, with all generosity; Flush had been beaten off by a servant, without a whip, because "it was right." There was no more to be said. Miss Barrett decided against him. "So he lay down on the floor at my feet," she wrote, "looking from under his eyebrows at me." But though Flush might look, Miss Barrett refused even to meet his eyes. There she lay on the sofa; there Flush lay on the floor.

And as he lay there, exiled, on the carpet, he went through one of those whirlpools of tumultuous emotion in which the soul is either dashed upon the rocks and splintered or, finding some tuft of foothold, slowly and painfully pulls itself up, regains dry land, and at last emerges on top of a ruined universe to survey a world created afresh on a different plan. Which was it to be—destruction or reconstruction? That was the question. The outlines only of his dilemma can be traced here; for his debate was silent. Twice Flush had done his utmost to kill his enemy; twice he had failed. And why had he failed, he asked himself? Because he loved Miss Barrett. Looking up at he· from under his eyebrows as she lay, severe and silent on the sofa, he knew that he must love her for ever. But things are not simple but complex. If he bit Mr. Browning he bit her too. Hatred is not hatred; hatred is also love. Here Flush shook his ears in an agony of perplexity. He turned uneasily on the floor. Mr. Browning was Miss Barrett—Miss Barrett was Mr. Browning; love is hatred and hatred is love. He stretched himself, whined and raised his head from the floor. The clock struck eight. For three hours and more he had been lying there, tossed from the horn of one dilemma to another.

Even Miss Barrett, severe, cold, implacable as she was, laid down her pen. "Wicked Flush!" she had been writing to Mr. Browning, ". . . if people like Flush, choose to behave like dogs savagely, they must take the consequences indeed, as dogs usually do! And *you*, so good and gentle to him! Anyone but *you*, would have said 'hasty words' at least." Really it would be a good plan, she thought, to buy a muzzle. And then she looked up and saw Flush. Something unusual in his look must have struck her. She paused. She laid down her pen. Once he had roused her with a kiss, and she had thought that he was Pan. He had eaten chicken and rice pudding soaked in cream. He had given up the sunshine for her sake. She called him to her and said she forgave him.

But to be forgiven, as if for a passing whim, to

78

be taken back again on to the sofa as if he had
learnt nothing in his anguish on the floor, as if he
were the same dog when in fact he differed totally,
was impossible. For the moment, exhausted as he
was, Flush submitted. A few days later, however,
a remarkable scene took place between him and
Miss Barrett which showed the depths of his emotions. Mr. Browning had been and gone; Flush
was alone with Miss Barrett. Normally he would
have leapt on to the sofa at her feet. But now, instead of jumping up as usual and claiming her caress, Flush went to what was now called "Mr.
Browning's armchair." Usually the chair was abhor-
rent to him; it still held the shape of his enemy. But
now, such was the battle he had won, such was the
charity that suffused him, that he not only looked at
the chair but, as he looked, "suddenly fell into a rapture." Miss Barrett, watching him intently, observed
this extraordinary portent. Next she saw him turn
his eyes towards a table. On that table still lay
the packet of Mr. Browning's cakes. He "reminded
me that the cakes you left were on the table." They
were now old cakes, stale cakes, cakes bereft of any
carnal seduction. Flush's meaning was plain. He had

79

refused to eat the cakes when they were fresh, because they were offered by an enemy. He would eat them now that they were stale, because they were offered by an enemy turned to friend, because they were symbols of hatred turned to love. Yes, he signified, he would eat them now. So Miss Barrett rose and took the cakes in her hand. And as she gave them to him she admonished him, "So I explained to him that *you* had brought them for him, and that he ought to be properly ashamed therefore for his past wickedness, and make up his mind to love you and not bite you for the future—and he was allowed to profit from your goodness to him." As he swallowed down the faded flakes of that distasteful pastry—it was mouldy, it was flyblown, it was sour—Flush solemnly repeated, in his own language, the words she had used—he swore to love Mr. Browning and not bite him for the future.

He was instantly rewarded—not by stale cakes, not by chicken's wings, not by the caresses that were now his, nor by the permission to lie once more on the sofa at Miss Barrett's feet. He was rewarded, spiritually; yet the effects were curiously physical. Like an iron bar corroding and festering and killing all natural life beneath it, hatred had lain all

these months across his soul. Now, by the cutting
of sharp knives and painful surgery, the iron had
been excised. Now the blood ran once more; the
nerves shot and tingled; flesh formed; Nature re-
joiced, as in spring. Flush heard the birds sing again;
he felt the leaves growing on the trees; as he lay on
the sofa at Miss Barrett's feet, glory and delight
coursed through his veins. He was with them, not
against them, now; their hopes, their wishes, their
desires were his. Flush could have barked in sympathy with Mr. Browning now. The short, sharp
words raised the hackles on his neck. "I need a week
of Tuesdays," Mr. Browning cried, "then a month
—a year—a life!" I, Flush echoed him, need a
month—a year—a life! I need all the things that
you both need. We are all three conspirators in the
most glorious of causes. We are joined in sympathy.
We are joined in hatred. We are joined in defiance
of black and beetling tyranny. We are joined in
love.—In short, all Flush's hopes now were set upon
some dimly apprehended but none the less certainly
emerging triumph, upon some glorious victory that
was to be theirs in common, when suddenly, without
a word of warning, in the midst of civilisation, se-

curity and friendship—he was in a shop in Vere Street with Miss Barrett and her sister: it was the morning of Tuesday the 1st of September—Flush was tumbled head over heels into darkness. The doors of a dungeon shut upon him. He was stolen.

4

Whitechapel

"THIS morning Arabel and I, and he with us,"
Miss Barrett wrote, "went in a cab to Vere Street
where we had a little business, and he followed
us as usual into a shop and out of it again, and
was at my heels when I stepped up into the carriage.
Having turned, I said 'Flush,' and Arabel looked
round for Flush—there was no Flush! He had been
caught up in that moment, from *under* the wheels,
do you understand?" Mr. Browning understood perfectly well. Miss Barrett had forgotten the chain;
therefore Flush was stolen. Such, in the year 1846,
was the law of Wimpole Street and its neighbourhood.

Nothing, it is true, could exceed the apparent
solidity and security of Wimpole Street itself. As far
as an invalid could walk or a bath-chair could trun-
dle nothing met the eye but an agreeable prospect
of four-storeyed houses, plate-glass windows and
mahogany doors. Even a carriage and pair, in the

course of an afternoon's airing, need not, if the coachman were discreet, leave the limits of decorum and respectability. But if you were not an invalid, if you did not possess a carriage and pair, if you were—and many people were—active and able-bodied and fond of walking, then you might see sights and hear language and smell smells, not a stone's-throw from Wimpole Street, that threw doubts upon the solidity even of Wimpole Street itself. So Mr. Thomas Beames found when about this time he took it into his head to go walking about London. He was surprised; indeed he was shocked. Splendid buildings raised themselves in Westminster, yet just behind them were ruined sheds in which human beings lived herded together above herds of cows—"two in each seven feet of space." He felt that he ought to tell people what he had seen. Yet how could one describe politely a bedroom in which two or three families lived above a cow-shed, when the cow-shed had no ventilation, when the cows were milked and killed and eaten under the bedroom? That was a task, as Mr. Beames found when he came to attempt it, that taxed all the resources of the English language. And yet he felt that he ought to describe what he had seen in the course of an

afternoon's walk through some of the most aristocratic parishes in London. The risk of typhus was
so great. The rich could not know what dangers
they were running. He could not altogether hold
his tongue when he found what he did find in Westminster and Paddington and Marylebone. For instance, here was an old mansion formerly belonging
to some great nobleman. Relics of marble mantel-
pieces remained. The rooms were panelled and the
banisters were carved, and yet the floors were rotten,
the walls dripped with filth; hordes of half-naked
men and women had taken up their lodging in the
old banqueting-halls. Then he walked on. Here an
enterprising builder had pulled down the old family
mansion. He had run up a jerry-built tenement house
in its place. The rain dripped through the roof and
the wind blew through the walls. He saw a child
dipping a can into a bright-green stream and asked
if they drank that water. Yes, and washed in it too,
for the landlord only allowed water to be turned on
twice a week. Such sights were the more surprising,
because one might come upon them in the most se-
date and civilised quarters of London—"the most
aristocratic parishes have their share." Behind Miss
Barrett's bedroom, for instance, was one of the worst

slums in London. Mixed up with that respectability was this filth. But there were certain quarters, of course, which had long been given over to the poor and were left undisturbed. In Whitechapel, or in a triangular space of ground at the bottom of the Tottenham Court Road, poverty and vice and misery had bred and seethed and propagated their kind for centuries without interference. A dense mass of aged buildings in St. Giles's was "wellnigh a penal settlement, a pauper metropolis in itself." Aptly enough, where the poor conglomerated thus, the settlement was called a Rookery. For there human beings swarmed on top of each other as rooks swarm and blacken tree-tops. Only the buildings here were not trees; they were hardly any longer buildings. They were cells of brick intersected by lanes which ran with filth. All day the lanes buzzed with half-dressed human beings; at night there poured back again into the stream the thieves, beggars, and prostitutes who had been plying their trade in the West End. The police could do nothing. No single wayfarer could do anything except hurry through as fast as he could and perhaps drop a hint, as Mr. Beames did, with many quotations, evasions and euphemisms, that all was not quite as it should be. Cholera would come, and perhaps the hint that cholera would give would not be quite so evasive.

But in the summer of 1846 that hint had not yet been given; and the only safe course for those who lived in Wimpole Street and its neighbourhood was to keep strictly within the respectable area and to lead your dog on a chain. If one forgot, as Miss Barrett forgot, one paid the penalty, as Miss Barrett was now to pay it. The terms upon which Wimpole Street lived cheek by jowl with St. Giles's were laid down. St. Giles's stole what St. Giles's could; Wimpole Street paid what Wimpole Street must. Thus Arabel at once "began to comfort me by showing how certain it was that I should recover him for ten pounds at most." Ten pounds, it was reckoned, was about the price that Mr. Taylor would ask for a cocker spaniel. Mr. Taylor was the head of the gang. As soon as a lady in Wimpole Street lost her dog she went to Mr. Taylor; he named his price, and it was paid; or if not, a brown paper parcel was delivered in Wimpole Street a few days later containing the head and paws of the dog. Such, at least, had been the experience of a lady in the neighbourhood who had tried to make terms with Mr. Taylor. But Miss Barrett of course intended to pay. Therefore when she got home she told her brother Henry, and Henry went to see Mr. Taylor that afternoon. He found him "smoking a cigar in a room with pictures"—Mr. Taylor was said to make an income of two or three thousand a year out of the dogs of Wimpole Street—and Mr. Taylor promised that he would confer with his "Society" and that the dog would be returned next day. Vexatious as it was, and especially annoying at a moment when Miss Barrett needed all her money, such were the inevitable consequences of forgetting in 1846 to keep one's dog on a chain.

But for Flush things were very different. Flush, Miss Barrett reflected, "doesn't know that we can recover him"; Flush had never mastered the principles of human society. "All this night he will howl and lament, I know perfectly," Miss Barrett wrote to Mr. Browning on the afternoon of Tuesday, the 1st September. But while Miss Barrett wrote to Mr. Browning, Flush was going through the most terrible experience of his life. He was bewildered in the extreme. One moment he was in Vere Street, among ribbons and laces; the next he was tumbled head over heels into a bag; jolted rapidly across streets, and at length was tumbled out—here. He

found himself in complete darkness. He found himself in chillness and dampness. As his giddiness left
him he made out a few shapes in a low dark room—
broken chairs, a tumbled mattress. Then he was
seized and tied tightly by the leg to some obstacle.
Something sprawled on the floor—whether beast or
human being, he could not tell. Great boots and
draggled skirts kept stumbling in and out. Flies
buzzed on scraps of old meat that were decaying on
the floor. Children crawled out from dark corners
and pinched his ears. He whined, and a heavy hand
beat him over the head. He cowered down on the
few inches of damp brick against the wall. Now he
could see that the floor was crowded with animals
of different kinds. Dogs tore and worried a festering
bone that they had got between them. Their ribs
stood out from their coats—they were half fam-
ished, dirty, diseased, uncombed, unbrushed; yet all
of them, Flush could see, were dogs of the highest
breeding, chained dogs, footmen's dogs, like himself.

He lay, not daring even to whimper, hour after
hour. Thirst was his worst suffering; but one sip of
the thick greenish water that stood in a pail near
him disgusted him; he would rather die than drink

91

another. Yet a majestic greyhound was drinking greedily. Whenever the door was kicked open he looked up. Miss Barrett—was it Miss Barrett? Had she come at last? But it was only a hairy ruffian, who kicked them all aside and stumbled to a broken chair upon which he flung himself. Then gradually the darkness thickened. He could scarcely make out what shapes those were, on the floor, on the mattress, on the broken chairs. A stump of candle was stuck on the ledge over the fireplace. A flare burnt in the gutter outside. By its flickering, coarse light Flush could see terrible faces passing outside, leering at the window. Then in they came, until the small crowded room became so crowded that he had to shrink back and lie even closer against the wall. These horrible monsters—some were ragged, others were flaring with paint and feathers—squatted on the floor; hunched themselves over the table. They began to drink; they cursed and struck each other. Out tumbled, from the bags that were dropped on the floor, more dogs—lap dogs, setters, pointers with their collars still on them; and a giant cockatoo that flustered and dashed its way from corner to corner shrieking "Pretty Poll," "Pretty Poll," with an accent that would have terrified its mistress, a widow in Maida Vale. Then the women's bags were opened, and out were tossed on to the table bracelets and rings and brooches such as Flush had seen Miss Barrett wear and Miss Henrietta. The demons pawed and clawed them; cursed and quarrelled over them. The dogs barked. The children shrieked, and the splendid cockatoo—such a bird as Flush had often seen pendant in a Wimpole Street window—shrieked "Pretty Poll! Pretty Poll!" faster and faster until a slipper was thrown at it and it flapped its great yellow-stained dove-grey wings in frenzy. Then the candle toppled over and fell. The room was dark. It grew steadily hotter and hotter; the smell, the heat, were unbearable; Flush's nose burnt; his coat twitched. And still Miss Barrett did not come.

Miss Barrett lay on her sofa in Wimpole Street. She was vexed; she was worried, but she was not seriously alarmed. Of course Flush would suffer; he would whine and bark all night; but it was only a question of a few hours. Mr. Taylor would name his sum; she would pay it; Flush would be returned.

The morning of Wednesday the 2nd September dawned in the rookeries of Whitechapel. The broken windows gradually became smeared with grey. Light fell upon the hairy faces of ruffians lying sprawled upon the floor. Flush woke from a trance that had veiled his eyes and once more realised the truth. This was now the truth—this room, these ruffians, these whining, snapping, tightly tethered dogs, this murk, this dampness. Could it be true that he had been in a shop, with ladies, among ribbons, only yesterday? Was there such a place as Wimpole Street? Was there a room where fresh water sparkled in a purple jar; had he lain on cushions; had he been given a chicken's wing nicely roasted; and had he been torn with rage and jealousy and bitten a man with yellow gloves? The whole of that life and its emotions floated away, dissolved, became unreal.

Here, as the dusty light filtered in, a woman heaved herself off a sack and staggered out to fetch beer. The drinking and the cursing began again. A fat woman held him up by his ears and pinched his ribs, and some odious joke was made about him —there was a roar of laughter as she threw him on the floor again. The door was kicked open and banged to. Whenever that happened he looked up. Was it Wilson? Could it possibly be Mr. Browning? Or Miss Barrett? But no—it was only another thief, another murderer; he cowered back at the mere sight of those draggled skirts, of those hard, horny boots. Once he tried to gnaw a bone that was hurled his way. But his teeth could not meet in stony flesh and the rank smell disgusted him. His thirst increased and he was forced to lap a little of the green water that had been spilt from the pail. But as Wednesday wore on and he became hotter and more parched and still more sore, lying on the broken boards, one thing merged in another. He scarcely noticed what was happening. It was only when the door opened that he raised his head and looked. No, it was not Miss Barrett.

Miss Barrett, lying on the sofa in Wimpole Street, was becoming anxious. There was some hitch in the proceedings. Taylor had promised that he would go down to Whitechapel on Wednesday afternoon and confer with "the Society." Yet Wednesday afternoon, Wednesday evening passed and still Taylor did not come. This could only mean, she supposed, that the price was going to be raised—which was inconvenient enough at the moment. Still, of course, she would have to pay it. "I must have my Flush, you know," she wrote to Mr. Browning. "I can't run any risk and bargain and haggle." So she lay on the sofa writing to Mr. Browning and listening for a knock at the door. But Wilson came up with the

95

letters; Wilson came up with the hot water. It was time for bed and Flush had not come.

Thursday the 3rd of September dawned in Whitechapel. The door opened and shut. The red setter who had been whining all night beside Flush on the floor was hauled off by a ruffian in a moleskin vest—to what fate? Was it better to be killed or to stay here? Which was worse—this life or that death? The racket, the hunger and the thirst, the reeking smells of the place—and once, Flush remembered, he had detested the scent of eau de cologne—were fast obliterating any clear image, any single desire. Fragments of old memories began turning in his head. Was that the voice of old Dr. Mitford shouting in the field? Was that Kerenhappock gossiping with the baker at the door? There was a rattling in the room and he thought he heard Miss Mitford tying up a bunch of geraniums. But it was only the wind—for it was stormy today—battering at the brown paper in the broken window pane. It was only some drunken voice raving in the gutter. It was only the old hag in the corner mumbling on and on and on as she fried a herring in a pan over a fire. He had been forgotten and deserted. No help was coming. No voice spoke to him—the parrots cried "Pretty

Poll, Pretty Poll" and the canaries kept up their senseless cheeping and chirping.

Then again evening darkened the room; the candle was stuck in its saucer; the coarse light flared outside; hordes of sinister men with bags on their backs, of garish women with painted faces, began to shuffle in at the door and to fling themselves down on the broken beds and tables. Another night had folded its blackness over Whitechapel. And the rain dripped steadily through a hole in the roof and drummed into a pail that had been stood to catch it. Miss Barrett had not come.

Thursday dawned in Wimpole Street. There was no sign of Flush—no message from Taylor. Miss Barrett was very much alarmed. She made enquiries. She summoned her brother Henry, and cross-examined him. She found out that he had tricked her. "The archfield" Taylor had come according to his promise the night before. He had stated his terms— six guineas for the Society and half a guinea for himself. But Henry, instead of telling her, had told Mr. Barrett, with the result, of course, that Mr. Barrett had ordered him not to pay, and to conceal the visit from his sister. Miss Barrett was "very vexed and angry." She bade her brother to go at once to Mr. Taylor and pay the money. Henry refused and "talked of Papa." But it was no use talking of Papa, she protested. While they talked of Papa, Flush would be killed. She made up her mind. If Henry would not go, she would go herself: ". . . if people won't do as I choose, I shall go down to-morrow morning, and bring Flush back with me," she wrote to Mr. Browning.

But Miss Barrett now found that it was easier to say this than to do it. It was almost as difficult for her to go to Flush as for Flush to come to her. All Wimpole Street was against her. The news that Flush was stolen and that Taylor demanded a ransom was now public property. Wimpole Street was determined to make a stand against Whitechapel. Blind Mr. Boyd sent word that in his opinion it would be "an awful sin" to pay the ransom. Her father and her brother were in league against her and were capable of any treachery in the interests of their class. But worst of all—far worse—Mr. Browning himself threw all his weight, all his eloquence, all his learning, all his logic, on the side of Wimpole Street and against Flush. If Miss Barrett gave way to Taylor, he wrote, she was giving way to tyranny; she was giving way to blackmailers; she was increasing

the power of evil over right, of wickedness over innocence. If she gave Taylor his demand, ". . .
how will the poor owners fare who have not money
enough for their dogs' redemption?" His imagination took fire; he imagined what he would say
if Taylor asked him even for five shillings; he would
say, "*You* are responsible for the proceedings of
your gang, and *you* I mark—don't talk nonsense to
me about cutting off heads or paws. Be as sure as
that I stand here and tell you, I will spend my whole
life in putting you down, the nuisance you declare
yourself—and by every imaginable means I will
be the death of you and as many of your accom-
plices as I can discover—but *you* I have discovered
and will never lose sight of. . . ." So Mr. Browning would have replied to Taylor if he had had the
good fortune to meet that gentleman. For indeed, he
went on, catching a later post with a second letter
that same Thursday afternoon, ". . . it is horrible
to fancy how all the oppressors in their several
ranks may, if they choose, twitch back to them by
the heartstrings after various modes the weak and
silent whose secret they have found out." He did
not blame Miss Barrett—nothing she did could be
anything but perfectly right, perfectly acceptable

99

to him. Still, he continued on Friday morning, "I think it lamentable weakness. . . ." If she encouraged Taylor who stole dogs, she encouraged Mr. Barnard Gregory who stole characters. Indirectly, she was responsible for all the wretches who cut their throats or fly the country because some blackmailer like Barnard Gregory took down a directory and blasted their characters. "But why write this string of truisms about the plainest thing in the world?" So Mr. Browning stormed and vociferated from New Cross twice daily.

Lying on her sofa, Miss Barrett read the letters. How easy it could have been to yield—how easy it would have been to say, "Your good opinion is worth more to me than a hundred cocker spaniels." How easy it would have been to sink back on her pillows and sigh, "I am a weak woman; I know nothing of law and justice; decide for me." She had only to refuse to pay the ransom; she had only to defy Taylor and his society. And if Flush were killed, if the dreadful parcel came and she opened it and out dropped his head and paws, there was Robert Browning by her side to assure her that she had done right and earned his respect. But Miss

Barrett was not to be intimidated. Miss Barrett took up her pen and refuted Robert Browning. It was all very well, she said, to quote Donne; to cite the case of Gregory; to invent spirited replies to Mr. Taylor—she would have done the same had Taylor struck her; had Gregory defamed her—would that they had! But what would Mr. Browning have done if the banditti had stolen her; had her in their power; threatened to cut off her ears and send them by post to New Cross? Whatever he would have done, her mind was made up. Flush was helpless. Her duty was to him. "But Flush, poor Flush, who has loved me so faithfully; have I a right to sacrifice *him* in his innocence, for the sake of any Mr. Taylor's guilt in the world?" Whatever Mr. Browning might say, she was going to rescue Flush, even if she went down into the jaws of Whitechapel to fetch him, even if Robert Browning despised her for doing so.

On Saturday, therefore, with Mr. Browning's letter lying open on the table before her, she began to dress. She read his "one word more—in all this, I labour against the execrable policy of the world's husbands, fathers, brothers and domineerers in general." So, if she went to Whitechapel she was siding against Robert Browning, and in favour of fathers, brothers and domineerers in general. Still, she went on dressing. A dog howled in the mews. It was tied up, helpless in the power of cruel men. It seemed to her to cry as it howled: "Think of Flush." She put on her shoes, her cloak, her hat. She glanced at Mr. Browning's letter once more. "I am about to marry you," she read. Still the dog howled. She left her room and went downstairs.

Henry Barrett met her and told her that in his opinion she might well be robbed and murdered if she did what she threatened. She told Wilson to call a cab. All trembling but submissive, Wilson obeyed. The cab came. Miss Barrett told Wilson to get in. Wilson, though convinced that death awaited her, got in. Miss Barrett told the cabman to drive to Manning Street, Shoreditch. Miss Barrett got in herself and off they drove. Soon they were beyond plate-glass windows, the mahogany doors and the area railings. They were in a world that Miss Barrett had never seen, had never guessed at. They were in a world where cows are herded under the bedroom floor, where whole families sleep in rooms with broken windows; in a world where water is turned on only twice a week, in a world where vice and poverty breed vice and poverty. They

had come to a region unknown to respectable cab-
drivers. The cab stopped; the driver asked his way at
a public-house. "Out came two or three men. 'Oh,
you want to find Mr. Taylor, I daresay!' " In this
mysterious world a cab with two ladies could only
come upon one errand, and that errand was already
known. It was sinister in the extreme. One of the
men ran into a house, and came out saying that Mr.
Taylor " 'wasn't at home! but wouldn't I get out?'
Wilson, in an aside of terror, entreated me not to
think of such a thing." A gang of men and boys
pressed round the cab. "Then wouldn't I see Mrs.
Taylor?" the man asked. Miss Barrett had no wish
whatever to see Mrs. Taylor; but now an immense
fat woman came out of the house, "fat enough to
have had an easy conscience all her life," and informed Miss Barrett that her husband was out:
"might be in in a few minutes, or in so many hours
—wouldn't I like to get out and wait?" Wilson
tugged at her gown. Imagine waiting in the house of
that woman! It was bad enough to sit in the cab
with the gang of men and boys pressing round them.
So Miss Barrett parleyed with the "immense femi-
nine bandit" from the cab. She said Mr. Taylor had
her dog; Mr. Taylor had promised to restore her

dog; would Mr. Taylor bring back her dog to Wimpole Street for certain that very day? "Oh yes, certainly," said the fat woman with the most gracious of smiles. She did believe that Taylor had left home precisely on that business. And she "poised her head to right and left with the most easy grace."

So the cab turned round and left Manning Street, Shoreditch. Wilson was of opinion that "we had escaped with our lives barely." Miss Barrett herself had been alarmed. "Plain enough it was that the gang was strong there. The society, the 'Fancy' . . . had their roots in the ground," she wrote. Her mind teemed with thoughts, her eyes were full of pictures. This, then, was what lay on the other side of Wimpole Street—these faces, these houses. She had seen more while she sat in the cab at the public-house than she had seen during the five years that she had lain in the back bedroom at Wimpole Street. "The faces of those men!" she exclaimed. They were branded on her eyeballs. They stimulated her imagination as "the divine marble presences," the busts on the bookcase, had never stimulated it. Here lived women like herself; while she lay on her sofa, reading, writing, they lived thus. But the cab was now trundling along between four-storeyed houses again.

Here were the familiar doors and windows: the avenue of pointed brick, the brass knockers, the regular curtains. Here was Wimpole Street and number fifty. Wilson sprang out—with what relief to find herself in safety can be imagined. But Miss Barrett, perhaps, hesitated a moment. She still saw "the faces of those men." They were to come before her again years later when she was sitting on a sunny balcony in Italy. They were to inspire the most vivid passages in *Aurora Leigh*. But now the butler had opened the door, and she went upstairs to her room again.

Saturday was the fifth day of Flush's imprisonment. Almost exhausted, almost hopeless, he lay panting in his dark corner of the teeming floor. Doors slammed and banged. Rough voices cried. Women screamed. Parrots chattered as they had chattered to widows in Maida Vale, but now evil old women merely cursed at them. Insects crawled in his fur, but he was too weak, too indifferent to shake his coat. All Flush's past life and its many scenes—Reading, the greenhouse, Miss Mitford, Mr. Kenyon, the bookcases, the busts, the peasants on the blind—had faded like snowflakes dissolved in a cauldron. If he still held to hope, it was to something nameless and formless; the featureless face of someone he still called "Miss Barrett." She still existed; all the rest of the world was gone; but she still existed, though such gulfs lay between them that it was impossible, almost, that she should reach him still. Darkness began to fall again, such darkness as seemed almost able to crush out his last hope —Miss Barrett.

In truth, the forces of Wimpole Street were still, even at this last moment, battling to keep Flush and Miss Barrett apart. On Saturday afternoon she lay and waited for Taylor to come, as the immensely fat woman had promised. At last he came, but he had not brought the dog. He sent up a message— Let Miss Barrett pay him six guineas on the spot, and he would go straight to Whitechapel and fetch the dog "on his word of honour." What "the archfiend" Taylor's word of honour might be worth, Miss Barrett could not say; but "there seemed no other way for it"; Flush's life was at stake; she counted out the guineas and sent them down to Taylor in the passage. But as ill luck would have it, as Taylor waited in the passage among the umbrellas, the engravings, the pile carpet and other valuable objects, Alfred Barrett came in. The sight of the archfiend Taylor actually in the house made him lose his temper. He burst into a rage. He called him "a swindler, and a liar and a thief." Thereupon Mr. Taylor cursed him back. What was far worse, he swore that "as he hoped to be saved, we should never see our dog again," and rushed out of the house. Next morning, then, the blood-stained parcel would arrive.

Miss Barrett flung on her clothes again and rushed downstairs. Where was Wilson? Let her call a cab. She was going back to Shoreditch instantly. Her family came running to prevent her. It was getting dark. She was exhausted already. The adventure was risky enough for a man in health. For her it was madness. So they told her. Her brothers, her sisters, all came round her threatening her, dissuading her, "crying out against me for being 'quite mad' and obstinate and wilful—I was called as many names as Mr. Taylor." But she stood her ground. At last they realised the extent of her folly. Whatever the risk might be they must give way to her. Septimus promised if Ba would return to her room "and be in good humour" that he would go to Taylor's himself and pay the money and bring back the dog.

So the dusk of the 5th of September faded into the blackness of night in Whitechapel. The door of the room was once more kicked open. A hairy man hauled Flush by the scruff of his neck out of his corner. Looking up into the hideous face of his old enemy, Flush did not know whether he was being taken to be killed or to be freed. Save for one phantom memory, he did not care. The man stooped. What were those great fingers fumbling at his throat for? Was it a knife or a chain? Stumbling, half blinded, on legs that staggered, Flush was led out into the open air.

In Wimpole Street Miss Barrett could not eat her dinner. Was Flush dead, or was Flush alive? She did not know. At eight o'clock there was a rap on the door; it was the usual letter from Mr. Browning. But as the door opened to admit the letter, something rushed in also: Flush. He made straight for his purple jar. It was filled three times over; and still he drank. Miss Barrett watched the dazed, bewildered dirty dog, drinking. "He was not so enthusiastic about seeing me as I expected," she remarked. No, there was only one thing in the world he wanted —clean water.

After all, Miss Barrett had but glanced at the faces of those men and she remembered them all her life. Flush had lain at their mercy in their midst for five whole days. Now as he lay on cushions once more, cold water was the only thing that seemed to have any substance, any reality. He drank continually. The old gods of the bedroom—the bookcase, the wardrobe, the busts—seemed to have lost their substance. This room was no longer the whole world; it was only a shelter; only a dell arched over by one trembling dock-leaf in a forest where wild beasts prowled and venomous snakes coiled; where behind every tree lurked a murderer ready to pounce. As he lay dazed and exhausted on the sofa at Miss Barrett's feet the howls of tethered dogs, the screams of birds in terror still sounded in his ears. When the door opened he started, expecting a hairy man with a knife—it was only Mr. Kenyon with a book; it was only Mr. Browning with his yellow gloves. But he shrank away from Mr. Kenyon and Mr. Browning now. He trusted them no longer. Behind those smiling, friendly faces were treachery and cruelty and deceit. Their caresses were hollow. He dreaded even walking with Wilson to the pillar-box. He would not stir without his chain. When they said, " 'Poor Flush, did the naughty men take you away?' he put up his head and moaned and yelled." A whip cracking sent him bolting down the area-steps into safety. Indoors he crept closer to Miss Barrett on the sofa. She alone had not deserted him. He still kept some faith in her. Gradually some substance returned to her. Exhausted, trembling, dirty and very thin he lay on the sofa at her feet.

As the days passed and the memory of Whitechapel grew fainter, Flush, lying close to Miss Barrett on the sofa, read her feelings more clearly than ever before. They had been parted; now they were together. Indeed they had never been so much akin. Every start she gave, every movement she made, passed through him too. And she seemed now to be perpetually starting and moving. The delivery of a parcel even made her jump. She opened the parcel; with trembling fingers she took out a pair of thick boots. She hid them instantly in the corner of the cupboard. Then she lay down as if nothing had happened; yet something had happened. When they were alone she rose and took a diamond necklace from a drawer. She took out the box that held Mr. Browning's letters. She laid the boots, the necklace and the letters all in a carpet-box together and then —as if she heard a step on the stair—she pushed the box under the bed and lay down hastily, covering herself with her shawl again. Such signs of secrecy and stealth must herald, Flush felt, some approaching crisis. Were they about to fly together? Were they about to escape together from this awful world of dog-stealers and tyrants? Oh, that it were possible! He trembled and whined with excitement; but in her low voice Miss Barrett bade him be quiet, and instantly he was quiet. She was very quiet too. She lay perfectly still on the sofa directly any of her brothers or sisters came in; she lay and talked to Mr. Barrett as she always lay and talked to Mr. Barrett.

But on Saturday, the 12th of September, Miss Barrett did what Flush had never known her do before. She dressed herself as if to go out directly after breakfast. Moreover, as he watched her dress, Flush knew perfectly well from the expression on her face that he was not to go with her. She was bound on secret business of her own. At ten Wilson came into the room. She also was dressed as if for a walk. They went out together; and Flush lay on the sofa and waited for their return. An hour or so later Miss Barrett came back alone. She did not look at him—she seemed to notice nothing. She drew off her gloves and for a moment he saw a gold ring shine on one of the fingers of her left hand. Then he saw her

111

slip the ring from her hand and hide it in the darkness of a drawer. Then she laid herself down as usual on the sofa. He lay by her side scarcely daring to breathe, for whatever had happened, and something had happened, it must at all costs be concealed.

At all costs the life of the bedroom must go on as usual. Yet everything was different. The very movement of the blind as it drew in and out seemed to Flush like a signal. And as the lights and shadows passed over the busts they too seemed to be hinting and beckoning. Everything in the room seemed to be aware of change; to be prepared for some event. And yet all was silent; all was concealed. The brothers and sisters came in and out as usual; Mr. Barrett came as usual in the evening. He looked as usual to see that the chop was finished, the wine drunk. Miss Barrett talked and laughed and gave no sign when anyone was in the room that she was hiding anything. Yet when they were alone she pulled out the box from under the bed and filled it hastily, stealthily, listening as she did so. And the signs of strain were unmistakable. On Sunday the church bells were ringing. "What bells are those?" somebody asked. "Marylebone Church bells," said

Miss Henrietta. Miss Barrett, Flush saw, went deadly white. But nobody else noticed anything.

So Monday passed, and Tuesday and Wednesday and Thursday. Over them all lay a blanket of silence, of eating and talking and lying still on the sofa as usual. Flush, tossing in uneasy sleep, dreamt that they were couched together under ferns and leaves in a vast forest; then the leaves were parted and he woke. It was dark; but in the darkness he saw Wilson come stealthily into the room, and take the box from beneath the bed and quietly carry it outside. This was on Friday night, the 18th of September. All Saturday morning he lay as one lies who knows that at any moment now a handkerchief may drop, a low whistle may sound and the signal will be given for death or for life. He watched Miss Barrett dress herself. At a quarter to four the door opened and Wilson came in. Then the signal was given—Miss Barrett lifted him in her arms. She rose and walked to the door. For a moment they stood looking round the room. There was the sofa and by it Mr. Browning's armchair. There were the busts and the tables. The sun filtered through the ivy leaves and the blind with peasants walking blew gently out. All was as usual. All seemed to expect a million more such moments to come to them; but for Miss Barrett and Flush this was the last. Very quietly Miss Barrett shut the door.

Very quietly they slipped downstairs, past the drawing-room, the library, the dining-room. All looked as they usually looked; smelt as they usually smelt; all were quiet as if sleeping in the hot September afternoon. On the mat in the hall Catiline lay sleeping too. They gained the front door and very quietly turned the handle. A cab was waiting outside.

"To Hodgson's," said Miss Barrett. She spoke almost in a whisper. Flush sat on her knee very still. Not for anything in the whole world would he have broken that tremendous silence.

5

CHAPTER FIVE

Italy

HOURS, days, weeks, it seemed of darkness and rattling; of sudden lights; and then long tunnels of gloom; of being flung this way and that; of being hastily lifted into the light and seeing Miss Barrett's face close, and thin trees and lines and rails and high light-specked houses—for it was the barbarous custom of railways in those days to make dogs travel in boxes—followed. Yet Flush was not afraid; they were escaping; they were leaving tyrants and dog-stealers behind them. Rattle, grind; grind, rattle as much as you like, he murmured, as the train flung him this way and that; only let us leave Wimpole Street and Whitechapel behind us. At last the light broadened; the rattling stopped. He heard birds singing and the sigh of trees in the wind. Or was it the rush of water? Opening his eyes at last, shaking his coat at last, he saw—the most astonishing sight conceivable. There was Miss Barrett on a rock in the midst of rushing waters. Trees bent over her;

the river raced round her. She must be in peril. With one bound Flush splashed through the stream and reached her. ". . . he is baptized in Petrarch's name," said Miss Barrett as he clambered up on to the rock by her side. For they were at Vaucluse; she had perched herself upon a stone in the middle of Petrarch's fountain.

Then there was more rattling and more grinding; and then again he was stood down on a stable floor; the darkness opened; light poured over him; he found himself alive, awake, bewildered, standing on reddish tiles in a vast bare room flooded with sunshine. He ran hither and thither smelling and touching. There was no carpet and no fireplace. There were no sofas, no armchairs, no bookcases, no busts. Pungent and unfamiliar smells tickled his nostrils and made him sneeze. The light, infinitely sharp and clear, dazzled his eyes. He had never been in a room—if this were indeed a room—that was so hard, so bright, so big, so empty. Miss Barrett looked smaller than ever sitting on a chair by a table in the midst. Then Wilson took him out of doors. He found himself almost blinded, first by the sun, then by the shadow. One-half of the street was burning hot; the other bitterly cold. Women went by wrapped in furs, yet they carried parasols to shade their heads. And the street was dry as bone. Though it was now the middle of November there was neither mud nor puddle to wet his paws or clot their feathers. There were no areas and no railings. There was none of that heady confusion of smells that made a walk down Wimpole Street or Oxford Street so distracting. On the other hand, the strange new smells that came from sharp stone corners, from dry yellow walls, were extraordinarily pungent and queer. Then from behind a black swinging curtain came an astonishing sweet smell, wafted in clouds; he stopped, his paws raised, to savour it; he made to follow it inside; he pushed in beneath the curtain. He had one glimpse of a booming light-sprinkled hall, very high and hollow; and then Wilson with a cry of horror, jerked him smartly back. They went on down the street again. The noise of the street was deafening. Everybody seemed to be shouting shrilly at the same moment. Instead of the solid and soporific hum of London there was a rattling and a crying, a jingling and a shouting, a cracking of whips and a jangling of bells. Flush leapt and jumped this way and that, and so did Wilson. They were forced on and off the pavement twenty times, to avoid a cart, a bullock, a troop of soldiers, a drove of goats. He felt younger, spryer than he had done these many years. Dazzled, yet exhilarated, he sank on the reddish tiles and slept more soundly than he had ever slept in the back bedroom at Wimpole Street upon pillows.

But soon Flush became aware of the more profound differences that distinguish Pisa—it was in Pisa that they were now settled—from London. The dogs were different. In London he could scarcely trot round to the pillar-box without meeting some pug dog, retriever, bulldog, mastiff, collie, Newfoundland, St. Bernard, fox terrier or one of the seven famous families of the Spaniel tribe. To each he gave a different name, and to each a different rank. But here in Pisa, though dogs abounded, there were no ranks; all—could it be possible?—were mongrels. As far as he could see, they were dogs merely—grey dogs, yellow dogs, brindled dogs, spotted dogs; but it was impossible to detect a single spaniel, collie, retriever or mastiff among them. Had the Kennel Club, then, no jurisdiction in Italy? Was the Spaniel Club unknown? Was there no law which decreed death to the topknot, which cherished the curled ear, protected the feathered foot, and insisted

absolutely that the brow must be domed but not
pointed? Apparently not. Flush felt himself like a
prince in exile. He was the sole aristocrat among a
crowd of *canaille*. He was the only pure-bred cocker
spaniel in the whole of Pisa.

For many years now Flush had been taught to
consider himself an aristocrat. The law of the purple
jar and of the chain had sunk deep into his soul.
It is scarcely surprising that he was thrown off his
balance. A Howard or a Cavendish set down among
a swarm of natives in mud huts can hardly be blamed
if now and again he remembers Chatsworth and
muses regretfully over red carpets and galleries
daubed with coronets as the sunset blazes down
through painted windows. There was an element,
it must be admitted, of the snob in Flush; Miss
Mitford had detected it years ago; and the sentiment, subdued in London among equals and superiors, returned to him now that he felt himself
unique. He became overbearing and impudent.
"Flush has grown an absolute monarch and barks
one distracted when he wants a door opened," Mrs.
Browning wrote. "Robert," she continued, "declares
that the said Flush considers him, my husband, to

121

be created for the especial purpose of doing him service, and really it looks rather like it."

"Robert," "my husband"—if Flush had changed, so had Miss Barrett. It was not merely that she called herself Mrs. Browning now; that she flashed the gold ring on her hand in the sun; she was changed, as much as Flush was changed. Flush heard her say, "Robert," "my husband," fifty times a day, and always with a ring of pride that made his hackles rise and his heart jump. But it was not her language only that had changed. She was a different person altogether. Now, for instance, instead of sipping a thimbleful of port and complaining of the headache, she tossed off a tumbler of Chianti and slept the sounder. There was a flowering branch of oranges on the dinner-table instead of one denuded, sour, yellow fruit. Then instead of driving in a barouche landau to Regent's Park she pulled on her thick boots and scrambled over rocks. Instead of sitting in a carriage and rumbling along Oxford Street, they rattled off in a ramshackle fly to the borders of a lake and looked at mountains; and when she was tired she did not hail another cab; she sat on a stone and watched the lizards. She delighted in the sun; she delighted in the cold. She threw pine

logs from the Duke's forest on to the fire if it froze.
They sat together in the crackling blaze and snuffed
up the sharp, aromatic scent. She was never tired of
praising Italy at the expense of England. ". . . our
poor English," she exclaimed, "want educating into
gladness. They want refining not in the fire but in
the sunshine." Here in Italy were freedom and life
and the joy that the sun breeds. One never saw men
fighting, or heard them swearing; one never saw the
Italians drunk;—"the faces of those men" in Shoreditch came again before her eyes. She was always
comparing Pisa with London and saying how much
she preferred Pisa. In the streets of Pisa pretty
women could walk alone; great ladies first emptied
their own slops and then went to Court "in a blaze
of undeniable glory." Pisa with all its bells, its mongrels, its camels, its pine woods, was infinitely pref-
erable to Wimpole Street and its mahogany doors
and its shoulders of mutton. So Mrs. Browning
every day, as she tossed off her Chianti and broke
another orange from the branch, praised Italy and
lamented poor, dull, damp, sunless, joyless, expensive, conventional England.

Wilson, it is true, for a time maintained her British balance. The memory of butlers and basements,

of front doors and curtains, was not obliterated from her mind without an effort. She still had the conscience to walk out of a picture gallery "struck back by the indecency of the Venus." And later, when she was allowed, by the kindness of a friend, to peep through a door at the glories of the Grand Ducal Court, she still loyally upheld the superior glory of St. James's. "It . . . was all very shabby," she reported, "in comparison with our English Court." But even as she gazed, the superb figure of one of the Grand Duke's bodyguard caught her eye. Her fancy was fired; her judgment reeled; her standards toppled. Lily Wilson fell passionately in love with Signor Righi, the guardsman.

And just as Mrs. Browning was exploring her new freedom and delighting in the discoveries she made, so Flush too was making his discoveries and exploring his freedom. Before they left Pisa—in the spring of 1847 they moved on to Florence—Flush had faced the curious and at first upsetting truth that the laws of the Kennel Club are not universal. He had brought himself to face the fact that light topknots are not necessarily fatal. He had revised his code accordingly. He had acted, at first with some hesitation, upon his new conception of

canine society. He was becoming daily more and
more democratic. Even in Pisa, Mrs. Browning noticed, ". . . he goes out every day and speaks Italian to the little dogs." Now in Florence the last
threads of his old fetters fell from him. The moment
of liberation came one day in the Cascine. As he
raced over the grass "like emeralds" with "the pheasants all alive and flying," Flush suddenly bethought
him of Regent's Park and its proclamation: Dogs
must be led on chains. Where was "must" now?
Where were chains now? Where were park-keepers
and truncheons? Gone, with the dog-stealers and
Kennel Clubs and Spaniel Clubs of a corrupt aristocracy! Gone with four-wheelers and hansom cabs!
with Whitechapel and Shoreditch! He ran, he raced;
his coat flashed; his eyes blazed. He was the friend
of all the world now. All dogs were his brothers. He
had no need of a chain in this new world; he had no
need of protection. If Mr. Browning was late in going for his walk—he and Flush were the best of
friends now—Flush boldly summoned him. He
"stands up before him and barks in the most imperious manner possible," Mrs. Browning observed with
some irritation—for her relations with Flush were
far less emotional now than in the old days; she no

longer needed his red fur and his bright eyes to give
her what her own experience lacked; she had found
Pan for herself among the vineyards and the olive
trees; he was there too beside the pine fire of an evening. So if Mr. Browning loitered, Flush stood up
and barked; but if Mr. Browning preferred to stay
at home and write, it did not matter. Flush was in-
dependent now. The wistarias and the laburnum
were flowering over walls; the Judas trees were
burning bright in the gardens; the wild tulips were
sprinkled in the fields. Why should he wait? Off
he ran by himself. He was his own master now.
". . . he goes out by himself, and stays hours together," Mrs. Browning wrote; ". . . knows every
street in Florence—will have his own way in everything. I am never frightened at his absence," she
added, remembering with a smile those hours of
agony in Wimpole Street and the gang waiting to
snatch him up under the horses' feet if she forgot
his chain in Vere Street. Fear was unknown in Florence; there were no dog-stealers here and, she may
have sighed, there were no fathers.

But, to speak candidly, it was not to stare at
pictures, to penetrate into dark churches and look
up at dim frescoes, that Flush scampered off when

the door of Casa Guidi was left open. It was to
enjoy something, it was in search of something de-
nied him all these years. Once the hunting horn
of Venus had blown its wild music over the Berkshire fields; he had loved Mr. Partridge's dog; she
had borne him a child. Now he heard the same
voice pealing down the narrow streets of Florence,
but more imperiously, more impetuously, after all
these years of silence. Now Flush knew what men
can never know—love pure, love simple, love entire;
love that brings no train of care in its wake; that
has no shame; no remorse; that is here, that is gone,
as the bee on the flower is here and is gone. Today the flower is a rose, tomorrow a lily; now it
is the wild thistle on the moor, now the pouched
and portentous orchid of the conservatory. So vari-
ously, so carelessly Flush embraced the spotted spaniel down the alley, and the brindled dog and the
yellow dog—it did not matter which. To Flush it
was all the same. He followed the horn wherever
the horn blew and the wind wafted it. Love was
all; love was enough. No one blamed him for his
escapades. Mr. Browning merely laughed—"Quite
disgraceful for a respectable dog like him"—when
Flush returned very late at night or early the next

morning. And Mrs. Browning laughed too, as Flush
flung himself down on the bedroom floor and slept
soundly upon the arms of the Guidi family inlaid in
scagliola.

For at Casa Guidi the rooms were bare. All those
draped objects of his cloistered and secluded days
had vanished. The bed was a bed; the wash-stand
was a wash-stand. Everything was itself and not another thing. The drawing-room was large and sprinkled with a few old carved chairs of ebony. Over the
fire hung a mirror with two cupids to hold the lights.
Mrs. Browning herself had discarded her Indian
shawls. She wore a cap made of some thin bright silk
that her husband liked. Her hair was brushed in a
new way. And when the sun had gone down and the
shutters had been raised she paced the balcony
dressed in thin white muslin. She loved to sit there
looking, listening, watching the people in the street.

They had not been long in Florence before one
night there was such a shouting and trampling in
the street that they ran to the balcony to see what
was happening. A vast crowd was surging under-
neath. They were carrying banners and shouting and
singing. All the windows were full of faces; all the
balconies were full of figures. The people in the

MRS. BROWNING

REPRODUCED BY PERMISSION OF THE
NATIONAL PORTRAIT GALLERY, LONDON

windows were tossing flowers and laurel leaves on
to the people in the street; and the people in the
street—grave men, gay young women—were kiss-
ing each other and raising their babies to the people
in the balconies. Mr. and Mrs. Browning leant over
the balustrade and clapped and clapped. Banner
after banner passed. The torches flashed their light
on them. "Liberty" was written on one; "The Union
of Italy" on another; and "The Memory of the
Martyrs" and "Viva Pio Nono" and "Viva Leo-
poldo Secondo"—for three and a half hours the
banners went by and the people cheered and Mr.
and Mrs. Browning stood with six candles burning
on the balcony, waving and waving. For some time
Flush too, stretched between them with his paws
over the sill, did his best to rejoice. But at last—
he could not conceal it—he yawned. "He confessed
at last that he thought they were rather long about
it," Mrs. Browning observed. A weariness, a doubt,
a ribaldry possessed him. What was it all for? he
asked himself. Who was this Grand Duke and what
had he promised? Why were they all so absurdly
excited?—for the ardour of Mrs. Browning, waving
and waving, as the banners passed, somehow annoyed him. Such enthusiasm for a Grand Duke was

exaggerated, he felt. And then, as the Grand Duke
passed, he became aware that a little dog had
stopped at the door. Seizing his chance when Mrs.
Browning was more than usually enthusiastic, he
slipped down from the balcony and made off.
Through the banners and the crowds he followed
her. She fled further and further into the heart of
Florence. Far away sounded the shouting; the cheers
of the people died down into silence. The lights of
the torches were extinguished. Only a star or two
shone in the ripples of the Arno where Flush lay with
the spotted spaniel by his side, couched in the shell
of an old basket on the mud. There tranced in love
they lay till the sun rose in the sky. Flush did not
return until nine next morning, and Mrs. Browning
greeted him rather ironically—he might at least, she
thought, have remembered that it was the first anni-
versary of her wedding day. But she supposed "he
had been very much amused." It was true. While she
had found an inexplicable satisfaction in the trampling of forty thousand people, in the promises of
Grand Dukes and the windy aspirations of banners,
Flush infinitely preferred the little dog at the door.

It cannot be doubted that Mrs. Browning and
Flush were reaching different conclusions in their

voyages of discovery—she a Grand Duke, he a spotted spaniel;—and yet the tie which bound them together was undeniably still binding. No sooner had Flush abolished "must" and raced free through the emerald grass of the Cascine gardens where the pheasants fluttered red and gold, than he felt a check. Once more he was thrown back on his haunches. At first it was nothing—a hint merely— only that Mrs. Browning in the spring of 1849 became busy with her needle. And yet there was something in the sight that gave Flush pause. She was not used to sew. He noted that Wilson moved a bed and she opened a drawer to put white clothes inside it. Raising his head from the tiled floor, he looked, he listened attentively. Was something once more about to happen? He looked anxiously for signs of trunks and packing. Was there to be another flight, another escape? But an escape to what, from what? There is nothing to be afraid of here, he assured Mrs. Browning. They need neither of them worry themselves in Florence about Mr. Taylor and dogs' heads wrapped up in brown paper parcels. Yet he was puzzled. The signs of change, as he read them, did not signify escape. They signified, much more mysteriously, expectance. Something, he felt, as he watched Mrs. Browning so composedly, yet silently and steadfastly, stitching in her low chair, was coming that was inevitable; yet to be dreaded. As the weeks went on, Mrs. Browning scarcely left the house. She seemed, as she sat there, to anticipate some tremendous event. Was she about to encounter somebody, like the ruffian Taylor, and let him rain blows on her alone and unaided? Flush quivered with apprehension at the thought. Certainly she had no intention of running away. No boxes were packed. There was no sign that anybody was about to leave the house—rather there were signs that somebody was coming. In his jealous anxiety Flush scrutinised each new-comer. There were many now—Miss Blagden, Mr. Landor, Hattie Hosmer, Mr. Lytton—ever so many ladies and gentlemen now came to Casa Guidi. Day after day Mrs. Browning sat there in her armchair quietly stitching.

Then one day early in March Mrs. Browning did not appear in the sitting-room at all. Other people came in and out; Mr. Browning and Wilson came in and out; and they came in and out so distractedly that Flush hid himself under the sofa. People were trampling up and down stairs, running and calling in low whispers and muted unfamiliar voices. They were moving upstairs in the bedroom. He crept further and further under the shadow of the sofa. He knew in every fibre of his body that some change was taking place—some awful event was happening. So he had waited, years ago, for the step of the hooded man on the staircase. And at last the door had opened and Miss Barrett had cried "Mr. Browning!" Who was coming now? What hooded man? As the day wore on, he was left completely alone. He lay in the drawing-room without food or drink; a thousand spotted spaniels might have sniffed at the door and he would have shrunk away from them. For as the hours passed he had an overwhelming sense that something was thrusting its way into the house from outside. He peeped out from beneath the flounces. The cupids holding the lights, the ebony chests, the French chairs, all looked thrust asunder; he himself felt as if he were being pushed up against the wall to make room for something that he could not see. Once he saw Mr. Browning, but he was not the same Mr. Browning; once Wilson, but she was changed too— as if they were both seeing the invisible presence that he felt.

At last Wilson, looking very flushed and untidy

but triumphant, took him in her arms and carried him upstairs. They entered the bedroom. There was a faint bleating in the shadowed room—something waved on the pillow. It was a live animal. Independently of them all, without the street door being opened, out of herself in the room, alone, Mrs. Browning had become two people. The horrid thing waved and mewed by her side. Torn with rage and jealousy and some deep disgust that he could not hide, Flush struggled himself free and rushed downstairs. Wilson and Mrs. Browning called him back; they tempted him with caresses; they offered him titbits; but it was useless. He cowered away from the disgusting sight, the repulsive presence, wherever there was a shadowy sofa or a dark corner. ". . . for a whole fortnight he fell into deep melancholy and was proof against all attentions lavished on him"—so Mrs. Browning, in the midst of all her other distractions, was forced to notice. And when we take, as we must, human minutes and hours and drop them into a dog's mind and see how the minutes swell into hours and the hours into days, we shall not exaggerate if we conclude that Flush's "deep melancholy" lasted six full months by the human clock. Many men and women have forgotten their hates and their loves in less.

But Flush was no longer the unschooled, untrained dog of Wimpole Street days. He had learnt his lesson. Wilson had struck him. He had been forced to swallow cakes that were stale when he might have eaten them fresh; he had sworn to love and not to bite. All this churned in his mind as he lay under the sofa; and at last he issued out. Again he was rewarded. At first, it must be admitted, the reward was insubstantial if not positively disagreeable. The baby was set on his back and Flush had to trot about with the baby pulling his ears. But he submitted with such grace, only turning round, when his ears were pulled, "to kiss the little bare, dimpled feet," that, before three months had passed, this helpless, weak, puling, muling lump had somehow come to prefer him, "on the whole"—so Mrs. Browning said—to other people. And then, strangely enough, Flush found that he returned the baby's affection. Did they not share something in common —did not the baby somehow resemble Flush in many ways? Did they not hold the same views, the same tastes? For instance, in the matter of scenery. To Flush all scenery was insipid. He had never, all these years, learnt to focus his eyes upon mountains. When they took him to Vallombrosa all the splendours of its woods had merely bored him. Now again, when the baby was a few months old, they went on another of those long expeditions in a travelling carriage. The baby lay on his nurse's lap; Flush sat on Mrs. Browning's knee. The carriage went on and on and on, painfully climbing the heights of the Apennines. Mrs. Browning was almost beside herself with delight. She could scarcely tear herself from the window. She could not find words enough in the whole of the English language to express what she felt. ". . . the exquisite, almost visionary scenery of the Apennines, the wonderful variety of shape and colour, the sudden transitions and vital individuality of those mountains, the chestnut forests dropping by their own weight into the deep ravines, the rocks cloven and clawed by the living torrents, and the hills, hill above hill, piling up their grand existences as if they did it themselves, changing colour in the effort"—the beauty of the Apennines brought words to birth in such numbers that they positively crushed each other out of existence. But the baby and Flush felt none of this stimulus, none of this inadequacy. Both were silent.

Flush drew "in his head from the window and didn't consider it worth looking at. . . . He has a supreme contempt for trees and hills or anything of that kind," Mrs. Browning concluded. The carriage rumbled on. Flush slept and the baby slept. Then at last there were lights and houses and men and women passing the windows. They had entered a village. Instantly Flush was all attention. ". . . his eyes were starting out of his head with eagerness; he looked east, he looked west, you would conclude that he was taking notes or preparing them." It was the human scene that stirred him, not beauty. Beauty, so it seems at least, had to be crystallised into a green or violet powder and puffed by some celestial syringe down the fringed channels that lay behind his nostrils before it touched Flush's senses; and then it issued not in words, but in a silent rapture. Where Mrs. Browning saw, he smelt; where she wrote, he snuffed.

Here, then, the biographer must perforce come to a pause. Where two or three thousand words are insufficient for what we see—and Mrs. Browning had to admit herself beaten by the Apennines: "Of these things I cannot give you any idea," she admitted—there are no more than two words and perhaps one-half for what we smell. The human nose is practically non-existent. The greatest poets in the world have smelt nothing but roses on the one hand, and dung on the other. The infinite gradations that lie between are unrecorded. Yet it was in the world of smell that Flush mostly lived. Love was chiefly smell; form and colour were smell; music and architecture, law, politics and science were smell. To him religion itself was smell. To describe his simplest experience with the daily chop or biscuit is beyond our power. Not even Mr. Swinburne could have said what the smell of Wimpole Street meant to Flush on a hot afternoon in June. As for describing the smell of a spaniel mixed with the smell of torches, laurels, incense, banners, wax candles and a garland of rose leaves crushed by a satin heel that has been laid up in camphor, perhaps Shakespeare, had he paused in the middle of writing *Antony and Cleopatra*— But Shakespeare did not pause. Confessing our inadequacy, then, we can but note that to Flush Italy, in these the fullest, the freest, the happiest years of his life, meant mainly a succession of smells. Love, it must be supposed, was gradually losing its appeal. Smell remained. Now that they were established in Casa Guidi again, all had their avocations. Mr. Browning wrote regularly in one room; Mrs.

Browning wrote regularly in another. The baby played in the nursery. But Flush wandered off into the streets of Florence to enjoy the rapture of smell. He threaded his path through main streets and back streets, through squares and alleys, by smell. He nosed his way from smell to smell; the rough, the smooth, the dark, the golden. He went in and out, up and down, where they beat brass, where they bake bread, where the women sit combing their hair, where the bird-cages are piled high on the causeway, where the wine spills itself in dark red stains on the pavement, where leather smells and harness and garlic, where cloth is beaten, where vine leaves tremble, where men sit and drink and spit and dice—he ran in and out, always with his nose to the ground, drinking in the essence; or with his nose in the air vibrating with the aroma. He slept in this hot patch of sun—how sun made the stone reek! he sought that tunnel of shade—how acid shade made the stone smell! He devoured whole bunches of ripe grapes largely because of their purple smell; he chewed and spat out whatever tough relic of goat or macaroni the Italian housewife had thrown from the balcony—goat and macaroni were raucous smells, crimson smells. He followed the

swooning sweetness of incense into the violet intrica-
cies of dark cathedrals; and, sniffing, tried to lap the
gold on the window-stained tomb. Nor was his sense
of touch much less acute. He knew Florence in its
marmoreal smoothness and in its gritty and cobbled
roughness. Hoary folds of drapery, smooth fingers
and feet of stone received the lick of his tongue, the
quiver of his shivering snout. Upon the infinitely
sensitive pads of his feet he took the clear stamp
of proud Latin inscriptions. In short, he knew Florence as no human being has ever known it; as Rus-
kin never knew it or George Eliot either. He knew
it as only the dumb know. Not a single one of his
myriad sensations ever submitted itself to the de-
formity of words.

But though it would be pleasant for the biographer to infer that Flush's life in late middle age
was an orgy of pleasure transcending all description; to maintain that while the baby day by day
picked up a new word and thus removed sensation
a little further beyond reach, Flush was fated to
remain for ever in a Paradise where essences exist
in their utmost purity, and the naked soul of things
presses on the naked nerve—it would not be true.
Flush lived in no such Paradise. The spirit, ranging

from star to star, the bird whose furthest flight over
polar snows or tropical forests never brings it
within sight of human houses and their curling
wood-smoke, may, for anything we know, enjoy such
immunity, such integrity of bliss. But Flush had
lain upon human knees and heard men's voices. His
flesh was veined with human passions; he knew all
grades of jealousy, anger and despair. Now in summer he was scourged by fleas. With a cruel irony
the sun that ripened the grapes brought also the
fleas. ". . . Savonarola's martyrdom here in Florence," wrote Mrs. Browning, "is scarcely worse than
Flush's in the summer." Fleas leapt to life in every
corner of the Florentine houses; they skipped and
hopped out of every cranny of the old stone; out of
every fold of old tapestry; out of every cloak, hat
and blanket. They nested in Flush's fur. They bit
their way into the thickest of his coat. He scratched
and tore. His health suffered; he became morose, thin
and feverish. Miss Mitford was appealed to. What
remedy was there, Mrs. Browning wrote anxiously,
for fleas? Miss Mitford, still sitting in her greenhouse at Three Mile Cross, still writing tragedies,
put down her pen and looked up her old prescrip-
tions—what Mayflower had taken, what Rosebud.

141

But the fleas of Reading die at a pinch. The fleas of Florence are red and virile. To them Miss Mitford's powders might well have been snuff. In despair Mr. and Mrs. Browning went down on their knees beside a pail of water and did their best to exorcise the pest with soap and scrubbing-brush. It was in vain. At last one day Mr. Browning, taking Flush for a walk, noticed that people pointed; he heard one man lay a finger to his nose and whisper "La rogna" (mange). As by this time "Robert is as fond of Flush as I am," to take his walk of an afternoon with a friend and to hear him thus stigmatised was intolerable. Robert, his wife wrote, "wouldn't bear it any longer." Only one remedy remained, but it was a remedy that was almost as drastic as the disease itself. However democratic Flush had become and careless of the signs of rank, he still remained what Philip Sidney had called him, a gentleman by birth. He carried his pedigree on his back. His coat meant to him what a gold watch inscribed with the family arms means to an impoverished squire whose broad acres have shrunk to that single circle. It was the coat that Mr. Browning now proposed to sacrifice. He called Flush to him and, "taking a pair of scissors, clipped him all over into the likeness of a lion."

As Robert Browning snipped, as the insignia of
a cocker spaniel fell to the floor, as the travesty of
quite a different animal rose round his neck, Flush
felt himself emasculated, diminished, ashamed.
What am I now? he thought, gazing into the glass.
And the glass replied with the brutal sincerity of
glasses, "You are nothing." He was nobody. Certainly he was no longer a cocker spaniel. But as he
gazed, his ears bald now, and uncurled, seemed to
twitch. It was as if the potent spirits of truth and
laughter were whispering in them. To be nothing—
is that not, after all, the most satisfactory state in
the whole world? He looked again. There was his
ruff. To caricature the pomposity of those who claim
that they are something—was that not in its way
a career? Anyhow, settle the matter as he might,
there could be no doubt that he was free from fleas.
He shook his ruff. He danced on his nude, attenu-
ated legs. His spirits rose. So might a great beauty,
rising from a bed of sickness and finding her face
eternally disfigured, make a bonfire of clothes and
cosmetics, and laugh with joy to think that she
need never look in the glass again or dread a lover's
coolness or a rival's beauty. So might a clergyman,
cased for twenty years in starch and broadcloth,

cast his collar into the dustbin and snatch the works of Voltaire from the cupboard. So Flush scampered off clipped all over into the likeness of a lion, but free from fleas. "Flush," Mrs. Browning wrote to her sister, "is wise." She was thinking perhaps of the Greek saying that happiness is only to be reached through suffering. The true philosopher is he who has lost his coat but is free from fleas.

But Flush had not long to wait before his newly-won philosophy was put to the test. Again in the summer of 1852 there were signs at Casa Guidi of one of those crises which, gathering soundlessly as a drawer opens or as a piece of string is left dangling from a box, are to a dog as menacing as the clouds which foretell lightning to a shepherd or as the rumours which foretell war to a statesman. Another change was indicated, another journey. Well, what of that? Trunks were hauled down and corded. The baby was carried out in his nurse's arms. Mr. and Mrs. Browning appeared, dressed for travelling. There was a cab at the door. Flush waited philosophically in the hall. When they were ready he was ready. Now that they were all seated in the carriage with one bound Flush sprang lightly in after them. To Venice, to Rome, to Paris—where were they going? All countries were equal to him now; all men were his brothers. He had learnt that lesson at last. But when finally he emerged from obscurity he had need of all his philosophy—he was in London.

Houses spread to right and left in sharp avenues of regular brick. The pavement was cold and hard beneath his feet. And there, issuing from a mahogany door with a brass knocker, was a lady bountifully apparelled in flowing robes of purple plush. A light wreath starred with flowers rested on her hair. Gathering her draperies about her, she glanced disdainfully up and down the street while a footman, stooping, let down the step of the barouche landau. All Welbeck Street—for Welbeck Street it was—was wrapped in a splendour of red light—a light not clear and fierce like the Italian light, but tawny and troubled with the dust of a million wheels, with the trampling of a million hooves. The London season was at its height. A pall of sound, a cloud of interwoven humming, fell over the city in one confluent growl. By came a majestic deerhound led on a chain by a page. A policeman swinging past with rhythmical stride, cast his bull's-eye from side to side. Odours of stew, odours of beef, odours of basting, odours of beef and cabbage rose from a

145

thousand basements. A flunkey in livery dropped a letter into a box.

Overcome by the magnificence of the metropolis, Flush paused for a moment with his foot on the doorstep. Wilson paused too. How paltry it seemed now, the civilisation of Italy, its Courts and its revolutions, its Grand Dukes and their bodyguards! She thanked God, as the policeman passed, that she had not married Signor Righi after all. And then a sinister figure issued from the public-house at the corner. A man leered. With one spring Flush bolted indoors.

For some weeks now he was closely confined to a lodging-house sitting-room in Welbeck Street. For confinement was still necessary. The cholera had come, and it is true that the cholera had done something to improve the condition of the Rookeries; but not enough, for still dogs were stolen and the dogs of Wimpole Street had still to be led on chains. Flush went into society, of course. He met dogs at the pillar-box and outside the public-house; and they welcomed him back with the inherent good breeding of their kind. Just as an English peer who has lived a lifetime in the East and contracted some of the habits of the natives—rumour hints indeed that he has turned Moslem and had a son by a Chinese washerwoman—finds, when he takes his place at Court, that old friends are ready enough to overlook these aberrations and he is asked to Chatsworth, though no mention is made of his wife and it is taken for granted that he will join the family at prayers— so the pointers and setters of Wimpole Street welcomed Flush among them and overlooked the condition of his coat. But there was a certain morbidity, it seemed to Flush now, among the dogs of London. It was common knowledge that Mrs. Carlyle's dog Nero had leapt from a top-storey window with the intention of committing suicide. He had found the strain of life in Cheyne Row intolerable, it was said. Indeed Flush could well believe it now that he was back again in Welbeck Street. The confinement, the crowd of little objects, the black-beetles by night, the bluebottles by day, the lingering odours of mutton, the perpetual presence on the sideboard of bananas—all this, together with the proximity of several men and women, heavily dressed and not often or indeed completely washed, wrought on his temper and strained his nerves. He lay for hours under the lodging-house chiffonier. It was impossible to run out of doors. The front door was always locked. He had to wait for somebody to lead him on a chain.

Two incidents alone broke the monotony of the weeks he spent in London. One day late that summer the Brownings went to visit the Rev. Charles Kingsley at Farnham. In Italy the earth would have been bare and hard as brick. Fleas would have been rampant. Languidly one would have dragged oneself from shadow to shadow, grateful even for the bar of shade cast by the raised arm of one of Donatello's statues. But here at Farnham there were fields of green grass; there were pools of blue water; there were woods that murmured, and turf so fine that the paws bounced as they touched it. The Brownings and the Kingsleys spent the day together. And once more, as Flush trotted behind them, the old trumpets blew; the old ecstasy returned—was it hare or was it fox? Flush tore over the heaths of Surrey as he had not run since the old days at Three Mile Cross. A pheasant went rocketing up in a spurt of purple and gold. He had almost shut his teeth on the tail feathers when a voice rang out. A whip cracked. Was it the Rev. Charles Kingsley who called him sharply to heel? At any rate he ran no more. The woods of Farnham were strictly preserved.

A few days later he was lying in the sitting-room at Welbeck Street, when Mrs. Browning came in dressed for walking and called him from under the chiffonier. She slipped the chain on to his collar and, for the first time since September 1846, they walked up Wimpole Street together. When they came to the door of number fifty they stopped as of old. Just as of old they waited. The butler just as of old was very slow in coming. At length the door opened. Could that be Catiline lying couched on the mat? The old toothless dog yawned and stretched himself and took no notice. Upstairs they crept as stealthily, as silently as once before they had come down. Very quietly, opening the doors as if she were afraid of what she might see there, Mrs. Browning went from room to room. A gloom descended upon her as she looked. ". . . they seemed to me," she wrote, "smaller and darker, somehow, and the furniture wanted fitness and convenience." The ivy was still tapping on the back bedroom window-pane. The painted blind still obscured the houses. Nothing had been changed. Nothing had happened all these years. So she went from room to room, sadly remembering. But long before she had finished her inspection, Flush was in a fever of anxiety. Suppose Mr. Barrett were to come in and find them? Suppose that with one frown, with one stare, he turned the key and locked them in the back bedroom for ever? At last Mrs. Browning shut the doors and went downstairs again very quietly. Yes, she said, it seemed to her that the house wanted cleaning.

After that, Flush had only one wish left in him— to leave London, to leave England for ever. He was not happy until he found himself on the deck of the Channel steamer crossing to France. It was a rough passage. The crossing took eight hours. As the steamer tossed and wallowed, Flush turned over in his mind a tumult of mixed memories—of ladies in purple plush, of ragged men with bags; of Regent's Park, and Queen Victoria sweeping past with outriders; of the greenness of English grass and the rankness of English pavements—all this passed through his mind as he lay on deck; and, looking up, he caught sight of a stern, tall man leaning over the rail.

"Mr. Carlyle!" he heard Mrs. Browning exclaim; whereupon—the crossing, it must be remembered, was a bad one—Flush was violently sick. Sailors came running with pails and mops. ". . . he was ordered off the deck on purpose, poor dog," said Mrs. Browning. For the deck was still English; dogs must not be sick on decks. Such was his last salute to the shores of his native land.

6

CHAPTER SIX

The End

FLUSH was growing an old dog now. The journey
to England and all the memories it revived had undoubtedly tired him. It was noticed that he sought
the shade rather than the sun on his return, though
the shade of Florence was hotter than the sun of
Wimpole Street. Stretched beneath a statue, couched
under the lip of a fountain for the sake of the few
drops that spurted now and again on to his coat, he
would lie dozing by the hour. The young dogs would
come about him. To them he would tell his stories of
Whitechapel and Wimpole Street; he would describe the smell of clover and the smell of Oxford
Street; he would rehearse his memories of one revo-
tion and another—how Grand Dukes had come and
Grand Dukes had gone; but the spotted spaniel
down the alley on the left—she goes on for ever,
he would say. Then violent Mr. Landor would hurry
by and shake his fist at him in mock fury; kind Miss
Isa Blagden would pause and take a sugared biscuit

from her reticule. The peasant women in the market-place made him a bed of leaves in the shadow of their baskets and tossed him a bunch of grapes now and then. He was known, he was liked by all Florence—gentle and simple, dogs and men.

But he was growing an old dog now, and he tended more and more to lie not even under the fountain—for the cobbles were too hard for his old bones—but in Mrs. Browning's bedroom where the arms of the Guidi family made a smooth patch of scagliola on the floor, or in the drawing-room under the shadow of the drawing-room table. One day shortly after his return from London he was stretched there fast asleep. The deep and dreamless sleep of old age was heavy on him. Indeed today his sleep was deeper even than usual, for as he slept the darkness seemed to thicken round him. If he dreamt at all, he dreamt that he was sleeping in the heart of a primeval forest, shut from the light of the sun, shut from the voices of mankind, though now and again as he slept he dreamt that he heard the sleepy chirp of a dreaming bird, or, as the wind tossed the branches, the mellow chuckle of a brooding monkey.

Then suddenly the branches parted; the light broke in—here, there, in dazzling shafts. Monkeys chattered; birds rose crying and calling in alarm. He started to his feet wide awake. An astonishing commotion was all round him. He had fallen asleep between the bare legs of an ordinary drawing-room table. Now he was hemmed in by the billowing of skirts and the heaving of trousers. The table itself, moreover, was swaying violently from side to side. He did not know which way to run. What on earth was happening? What in Heaven's name possessed the drawing-room table? He lifted up his voice in a prolonged howl of interrogation.

To Flush's question no satisfactory answer can here be given. A few facts, and those of the baldest, are all that can be supplied. Briefly, then, it would appear that early in the nineteenth century the Countess of Blessington had bought a crystal ball from a magician. Her ladyship "never could understand the use of it"; indeed she had never been able to see anything in the ball except crystal. After her death, however, there was a sale of her effects and the ball came into the possession of others who "looked deeper, or with purer eyes," and saw other things in the ball besides crystal. Whether Lord Stanhope was the purchaser, whether it was he who looked "with purer eyes," is not stated. But certainly by the year 1852 Lord Stanhope was in possession of a crystal ball and Lord Stanhope had only to look into it to see among other things "the spirits of the sun." Obviously this was not a sight that a hospitable nobleman could keep to himself, and Lord Stanhope was in the habit of displaying his ball at luncheon parties and of inviting his friends to see the spirits of the sun also. There was something strangely delightful—except indeed to Mr. Chorley—in the spectacle; balls became the rage; and luckily a London optician soon discovered that he could make them, without being either an Egyptian or a magician, though naturally the price of English crystal was high. Thus many people in the early 'fifties became possessed of balls, though "many persons," Lord Stanhope said, "use the balls, without the moral courage to confess it." The prevalence of spirits in London indeed became so marked that some alarm was felt; and Lord Stanley suggested to Sir Edward Lytton "that the Government should appoint a committee of investigation so as to get as far as possible at the facts." Whether the rumour of an approaching Government committee alarmed the spirits, or whether spirits, like bodies, tend to multiply in close confinement, there can be no doubt that the spirits began to show signs of restlessness, and, escaping in vast numbers, took up their residence in the legs of tables. Whatever the motive, the policy was successful. Crystal balls were expensive; almost everybody owns a table. Thus when Mrs. Browning returned to Italy in the winter of 1852 she found that the spirits had preceded her; the tables of Florence were almost universally infected. "From the Legation to the English chemists," she wrote, "people are 'serving tables' . . . everywhere. When people gather round a table it isn't to play whist." No, it was to decipher messages conveyed by the legs of tables. Thus if asked the age of a child, the table "expresses itself intelligently by knocking with its legs, responses according to the alphabet." And if a table could tell you that your own child was four years old, what limit was there to its capacity? Spinning tables were advertised in shops. The walls were placarded with advertisements of wonders *"scoperte a Livorno."* By the year 1854, so rapidly did the movement spread, "four hundred thousand families in America had given their names . . . as actually in enjoyment of spiritual intercourse." And from England the news came that Sir Edward Bulwer-Lytton had imported "several of the American rap-

ping spirits" to Knebworth, with the happy result—
so little Arthur Russell was informed when he be-
held a "strange-looking old gentleman in a shabby
dressing-gown" staring at him at breakfast—that
Sir Edward Bulwer-Lytton believed himself invisible.

When Mrs. Browning first looked into Lord Stanhope's crystal ball at a luncheon party she saw
nothing—except indeed that it was a remarkable
sign of the times. The spirit of the sun indeed told
her that she was about to go to Rome; but as she was
not about to go to Rome, she contradicted the spirits
of the sun. "But," she added, with truth, "I love the
marvellous." She was nothing if not adventurous.
She had gone to Manning Street at the risk of her
life. She had discovered a world that she had never
dreamt of within half an hour's drive from Wimpole Street. Why should there not be another world
only half a moment's flight from Florence—a better
world, a more beautiful world, where the dead live,
trying in vain to reach us? At any rate she would
take the risk. And so she sat herself down at the
table too. And Mr. Lytton, the brilliant son of an
invisible father, came; and Mr. Frederick Tennyson,
and Mr. Powers and M. Villari—they all sat at the

table and then when the table had done kicking, they sat on drinking tea and eating strawberries and cream, with "Florence dissolving in the purple of the hills and the stars looking on," talking and talking: ". . . what stories we told, and what miracles we swore to! Oh, we are believers here, Isa, except Robert. . . ." Then in burst deaf Mr. Kirkup with his bleak white beard. He had come round simply to exclaim, "There is a spiritual world—there is a future state. I confess it. I am convinced at last." And when Mr. Kirkup, whose creed had always been "the next thing to atheism," was converted merely because, in spite of his deafness, he had heard "three taps so loud that they made him leap," how could Mrs. Browning keep her hands off the table? "You know I am rather a visionary and inclined to knock round at all the doors of the present world to try to get out," she wrote. So she summoned the faithful to Casa Guidi; and there they sat with their hands on the drawing-room table, trying to get out.

Flush started up in the wildest apprehension. The skirts and the trousers were billowing round him; the table was standing on one leg. But whatever the ladies and gentlemen round the table could hear and see, Flush could hear and see nothing. True, the

161

table was standing on one leg, but so tables will if
you lean hard on one side. He had upset tables
himself and been well scolded for it. But now there
was Mrs. Browning with her great eyes wide open
staring as if she saw something marvellous outside.
Flush rushed to the balcony and looked over. Was
there another Grand Duke riding by with banners
and torches? Flush could see nothing but an old beggar woman crouched at the corner of the street over
her basket of melons. Yet clearly Mrs. Browning
saw something; clearly she saw something that was
very wonderful. So in the old Wimpole Street days
she had wept once without any reason that he could
see; and again she had laughed, holding up a blotted scrawl. But this was different. There was something in her look now that frightened him. There
was something in the room, or in the table, or in
the petticoats and trousers, that he disliked exceed-
ingly.

As the weeks passed, this preoccupation of Mrs.
Browning's with the invisible grew upon her. It
might be a fine hot day, but instead of watching
the lizards slide in and out of the stones, she would
sit at the table; it might be a dark starry night, but
instead of reading in her book, or passing her hand

over paper, she would call, if Mr. Browning were
out, for Wilson, and Wilson would come yawning.
Then they would sit at the table together until that
article of furniture, whose chief function it was to
provide shade, kicked on the floor, and Mrs. Browning exclaimed that it was telling Wilson that she
would soon be ill. Wilson replied that she was only
sleepy. But soon Wilson herself, the implacable, the
upright, the British, screamed and went into a faint,
and Mrs. Browning was rushing hither and thither
to find "the hygienic vinegar." That, to Flush, was
a highly unpleasant way of spending a quiet evening. Better far to sit and read one's book.

Undoubtedly the suspense, the intangibile but disagreeable odour, the kicks and the screams and the
vinegar, told upon Flush's nerves. It was all very
well for the baby, Penini, to pray "that Flush's hair
may grow"; that was an aspiration that Flush could
understand. But this form of prayer which required
the presence of evil-smelling, seedy-looking men and
the antics of a piece of apparently solid mahogany,
angered him much as they angered that robust, sensible, well-dressed man, his master. But far worse
than any smell to Flush, far worse than any antics,
was the look on Mrs. Browning's face when she

gazed out of the window as if she were seeing something that was wonderful when there was nothing. Flush stood himself in front of her. She looked through him as if he were not there. That was the cruellest look she had ever given him. It was worse than her cold anger when he bit Mr. Browning in the leg; worse than her sardonic laughter when the door shut upon his paw in Regent's Park. There were moments indeed when he regretted Wimpole Street and its tables. The tables at No. 50 had never tilted upon one leg. The little table with the ring round it that held her precious ornaments had always stood perfectly still. In those far-off days he had only to leap on her sofa and Miss Barrett started wide-awake and looked at him. Now, once more, he leapt on to her sofa. But she did not notice him. She was writing. She paid no attention to him. She went on writing—"also, at the request of the medium, the spiritual hands took from the table a garland which lay there, and placed it upon my head. The particular hand which did this was of the largest human size, as white as snow, and very beautiful. It was as near to me as this hand I write with, and I saw it as distinctly." Flush pawed her sharply. She looked through him as if he were invisible. He leapt off the sofa and ran downstairs into the street.

It was a blazing hot afternoon. The old beggar woman at the corner had fallen asleep over her melons. The sun seemed droning in the air. Keeping to the shady side of the street, Flush trotted along the well-known ways to the market-place. The whole square was brilliant with awnings and stalls and bright umbrellas. The market women were sitting beside baskets of fruit; pigeons were fluttering, bells were pealing, whips were cracking. The many-coloured mongrels of Florence were running in and out sniffing and pawing. All was as brisk as a beehive and as hot as an oven. Flush sought the shade. He flung himself down beside his friend Catterina, under the shadow of her great basket. A brown jar of red and yellow flowers cast a shadow beside it. Above them a statue, holding his right arm outstretched, deepened the shade to violet. Flush lay there in the cool, watching the young dogs busy with their own affairs. They were snarling and biting, stretching and tumbling, in all the abandonment of youthful joy. They were chasing each other in and out, round and round, as he had once chased the spotted spaniel in the alley. His thoughts turned to Reading for a moment—to Mr. Partridge's spaniel, to his first love, to the ecstasies and innocences of youth. Well, he had had his day. He did not grudge them theirs. He had found the world a pleasant place to live in. He had no quarrel with it now. The market woman scratched him behind the ear. She had often cuffed him for stealing a grape, or for some other misdemeanour; but he was old now; and she was old. He guarded her melons and she scratched his ear. So she knitted and he dozed. The flies buzzed on the great pink melon that had been sliced open to show its flesh.

The sun burnt deliciously through the lily leaves, and through the green and white umbrella. The marble statue tempered its heat to a champagne freshness. Flush lay and let it burn through his fur to the naked skin. And when he was roasted on one side he turned over and let the sun roast the other. All the time the market people were chattering and bargaining; market women were passing; they were stopping and fingering the vegetables and the fruit. There was a perpetual buzz and hum of human voices such as Flush loved to listen to. After a time he drowsed off under the shadow of the lilies. He slept as dogs sleep when they are dreaming. Now his legs twitched —was he dreaming that he hunted rabbits in Spain?

166

Was he coursing up a hot hill-side with dark men shouting "Span! Span!" as the rabbits darted from the brushwood? Then he lay still again. And now he yelped, quickly, softly, many times in succession. Perhaps he heard Dr. Mitford egging his greyhounds on to the hunt at Reading. Then his tail wagged sheepishly. Did he hear old Miss Mitford cry, "Bad dog! Bad dog!" as he slunk back to her, where she stood among the turnips waving her umbrella? And then he lay for a time snoring, wrapt in the deep sleep of happy old age. Suddenly every muscle in his body twitched. He woke with a violent start. Where did he think he was? In Whitechapel among the ruffians? Was the knife at his throat again?

Whatever it was, he woke from his dream in a state of terror. He made off as if he were flying to safety, as if he were seeking refuge. The market women laughed and pelted him with rotten grapes and called him back. He took no notice. Cart-wheels almost crushed him as he darted through the streets— the men standing up to drive cursed him and flicked him with their whips. Half-naked children threw pebbles at him and shouted *"Matta! Matta!"* as he fled past. Their mothers ran to the door and caught them back in alarm. Had he then gone mad? Had the sun turned his brain? Or had he once more heard the hunting horn of Venus? Or had one of the American rapping spirits, one of the spirits that live in table legs, got possession of him at last? Whatever it was, he went in a bee-line up one street and down another until he reached the door of Casa Guidi. He made his way straight upstairs and went straight into the drawing-room.

Mrs. Browning was lying, reading, on the sofa. She looked up, startled, as he came in. It was not a spirit—it was only Flush. She laughed. Then, as he leapt on to the sofa and thrust his face into hers, the words of her own poem came into her mind:

> You see this dog. It was but yesterday
> I mused forgetful of his presence here
> Till thought on thought drew downward tear on tear,
> When from the pillow, where wet-cheeked I lay,
> A head as hairy as Faunus, thrust its way
> Right sudden against my face,—two golden-clear
> Great eyes astonished mine,—a drooping ear
> Did flap me on either cheek to dry the spray!
> I started first, as some Arcadian,
> Amazed by goatly god in twilight grove;
> But, as the bearded vision closelier ran
> My tears off, I knew Flush, and rose above
> Surprise and sadness,—thanking the true Pan,
> Who, by low creatures, leads to heights of love.

She had written that poem one day years ago in Wimpole Street when she was very unhappy. Years had passed; now she was happy. She was growing old now and so was Flush. She bent down over him for a moment. Her face with its wide mouth and its great eyes and its heavy curls was still oddly like his. Broken asunder, yet made in the same mould, each, perhaps, completed what was dormant in the other. But she was woman; he was dog. Mrs. Browning went on reading. Then she looked at Flush again. But he did not look at her. An extraordinary change had come over him. "Flush!" she cried. But he was silent. He had been alive; he was now dead. That was all. The drawing-room table, strangely enough, stood perfectly still.

Authorities

IT MUST be admitted that there are very few authorities for the foregoing biography. But the reader who would like to check the facts or to pursue the subject further is referred to:

To Flush, My Dog.   }   Poems by
Flush, or Faunus.   }   Elizabeth Barrett Browning.

The Letters of Robert Browning and Elizabeth Barrett Browning. 2 vols.

The Letters of Elizabeth Barrett Browning, edited by Frederick Kenyon. 2 vols.

The Letters of Elizabeth Barrett Browning addressed to Richard Hengist Horne, edited by S. R. Townshend Mayer. 2 vols.

Elizabeth Barrett Browning: letters to her sister 1846-1859, edited by Leonard Huxley, LL.D.

Elizabeth Barrett Browning in her Letters, by Percy Lubbock.

References to Flush are to be found in the *Letters of Mary Russell Mitford,* edited by H. Chorley. 2 vols.

For an account of London Rookeries, *The Rookeries of London,* by Thomas Beames, 1850, may be consulted.

Notes

P. 28. "painted fabric." Miss Barrett says, "I had a transparent blind put up in my open window." She adds, "papa insults me with the analogy of a back window in a confectioner's shop, but is obviously moved when the sunshine lights up the castle, notwithstanding." Some hold that the castle, etc., was painted on a thin metallic substance; others that it was a muslin blind richly embroidered. There seems no certain way of settling the matter.

P. 49. "Mr. Kenyon mumbled slightly because he had lost two front teeth." There are elements of exaggeration and conjecture here. Miss Mitford is the authority. She is reported to have said in conversation with Mr. Horne, "Our dear friend, you are aware, never sees anybody but the members of her own family, and one or two others. She has a high opinion of the skill in *reading* as well as the fine taste, of Mr. ——, and she gets him to read her new poems aloud to her. . . . So Mr. —— stands upon the hearth-rug, and uplifts the MS., and his voice, while our dear friend lies folded up in Indian shawls upon her sofa, with her long black tresses streaming over her bent-down head, all attention. Now, dear Mr. —— has lost a front tooth—not quite a front one, but a side front one—and this, you see, causes a defective utterance . . . an amiable indistinctness, a vague softening of syllables into each other, so that silence and ilence would really sound very like one another. . . ." There can be little doubt that Mr. —— was Mr. Kenyon; the blank was necessitated by the peculiar delicacy of the Victorians with regard to teeth. But more important questions affecting English literature are involved. Miss Barrett has long been accused of a defective ear. Miss Mitford maintains that Mr. Kenyon should rather be accused of defective teeth. On the other hand, Miss Barrett herself maintained that her rhymes had nothing to do with his lack of teeth or with her lack of ear. "A great deal of attention," she wrote, "—far more than it would have taken to rhyme with complete accuracy—have I given to the subject of rhymes and have determined in cold blood to hazard some experiments." Hence she rhymed "angels" with "candles," "heaven" with "unbelieving," and "islands" with "silence"—in cold blood. It is of course for the professors to decide; but anybody who has studied Mrs. Browning's character and her actions will be inclined to take the view that she was a wilful breaker of rules whether of art or of love, and so to convict her of some complicity in the development of modern poetry.

P. 64. "yellow gloves." It is recorded in Mrs. Orr's Life of Browning that he wore lemon-coloured gloves. Mrs. Bridell-Fox, meeting him in 1835-6, says, "he was then slim and dark, and very handsome, and—may I hint it—just a trifle of a dandy, addicted to lemon-coloured kid gloves and such things."

P. 82. "He was stolen." As a matter of fact, Flush was stolen three times; but the unities seem to require that the three stealings shall be compressed into one. The total sum paid by Miss Barrett to the dog-stealers was £20.

P. 105. "The faces of those men were to come back to her on a sunny balcony in Italy." Readers of *Aurora Leigh*—but since such persons are non-existent it must be explained that Mrs. Browning wrote a poem of this name, one of the most vivid passages in which (though it suffers from the distortion natural to an artist who sees the object once only from a four-wheeler, with Wilson tugging at her skirts) is the description of a London slum. Clearly Mrs. Browning possessed a fund of curiosity as to human life which was by no means satisfied by the busts of Homer and Chaucer on the washing-stand in the bedroom.

P. 124. "Lily Wilson fell in love with Signor Righi, the guardsman." The life of Lily Wilson is extremely obscure and thus cries aloud for the services of a biographer. No human figure in the Browning letters, save the principals, more excites our curiosity and baffles it. Her Christian name was Lily, her surname Wilson. That is all we know of her birth and upbringing. Whether she was the daughter of a farmer in the neighbourhood of Hope End, and became favourably known to the Barrett cook by the decency of her demeanour and the cleanliness of her apron, so much so that when she came up to the great house on some errand, Mrs. Barrett made an excuse to come into the room just then and thought so well of her that she appointed her to be Miss Elizabeth's maid; or whether she was a Cockney; or whether she was from Scotland—it is impossible to say. At any rate she was in service with Miss Barrett in the year 1846. She was "an expensive servant"—her wages were £16 a year. Since she spoke almost as seldom as Flush, the outlines of her character are little known; and since Miss Barrett never wrote a poem about her, her appearance is far less familiar than his. Yet it is clear from indications in the letters that she was in the beginning one of those demure, almost inhumanly correct British maids who were at that time the glory of the British basement. It is obvious that Wilson was a stickler for rights and ceremonies. Wilson undoubtedly revered "the room"; Wilson would have been the first to insist that under servants must eat their pudding in one place, upper servants in another. All this is implicit in the remark she made when she beat Flush with her hand "because it is right." Such respect for convention, it need hardly be said, breeds extreme horror of any breach of it; so that when Wilson was confronted with the lower orders in Manning Street she was far more alarmed, and far more certain that the dog-stealers were murderers, than Miss Barrett was. At the same time the heroic way in which she overcame her terror and went with Miss Barrett in the cab shows how deeply the other convention of loyalty to her mistress was ingrained in her. Where Miss Barrett went, Wilson must go too. This principle was triumphantly demonstrated by her conduct at the time of the elopement. Miss Barrett had been doubtful of Wilson's courage; but her doubts were unfounded. "Wilson," she wrote—and these were the last words she ever wrote to Mr. Browning as Miss Barrett—"has been perfect to me. And *I* . . . calling her 'timid' and afraid of her timidity! I begin to think that none are so bold as the timid, when they are fairly roused." It is worth, parenthetically, dwelling for a second on the extreme precariousness of a servant's life. If Wilson had not gone with Miss Barrett, she would have been, as Miss Barrett knew, "turned into the street before sunset," with only a few shillings, presumably, saved from her sixteen pounds a year. And what then would have been her fate? Since English fiction in the 'forties scarcely deals with the lives of ladies' maids, and biography had not then cast its searchlight so low, the question must remain a question. But Wilson took the plunge. She declared that she would "go anywhere in the world with me." She left the basement, the room, the whole of that world of Wimpole Street, which to Wilson meant all civilisation, all right thinking and decent living, for the wild debauchery and irreligion of a foreign land. Nothing is more curious than to observe the conflict that took place in Italy between Wilson's English gentility and her natural passions. She derided the Italian Court; she was shocked by Italian pictures. But, though "she was struck back by the indecency of the Venus," Wilson, greatly to her credit, seems to have bethought her that women are naked when they take their clothes off. Even I myself, she may have thought, am naked for two or three seconds daily. And so "She thinks she shall try again, and the troublesome modesty may subside, who knows?" That it did subside rapidly is plain. Soon she not merely approved of Italy; she had fallen in love with Signor Righi of the Grand Ducal bodyguard—"all highly respectable and moral men, and some six feet high"—was wearing an engagement ring; was dismissing a London suitor; and was learning to speak Italian. Then the clouds descend again; when they lift they show us Wilson deserted —"the faithless Righi had backed out of his engagement to Wilson." Suspicion attaches to his brother, a wholesale haberdasher at Prato. When Righi resigned from the Ducal bodyguard, he became, on his

brother's advice, a retail haberdasher at Prato.
Whether his position required a knowledge of haber-
dashery in his wife, whether one of the girls of Prato
could supply it, it is certain that he did not write to
Wilson as often as he should have done. But what
conduct it was on the part of this highly respectable
and moral man that led Mrs. Browning to exclaim in
1850, "[Wilson] is *over* it completely, which does
the greatest credit to her good sense and rectitude of
character. How could she continue to love such a
man?"—why Righi had shrunk to "such a man" in
so short a time, it is impossible to say. Deserted by
Righi, Wilson became more and more attached to
the Browning family. She discharged not only the
duties of a lady's maid, but cooked knead cakes,
made dresses, and became a devoted nurse to Penini,
the baby; so that in time the baby himself exalted
her to the rank of the family, where she justly be-
longed, and refused to call her anything but Lily.
In 1855 Wilson married Romagnoli, the Brownings'
manservant, "a good tender-hearted man"; and for
some time the two kept house for the Brownings. But
in 1859 Robert Browning "accepted office as Landor's guardian," an office of great delicacy and re-
sponsibility, for Landor's habits were difficult; "of

restraint he has not a grain," Mrs. Browning wrote, "and of suspiciousness many grains." In these circumstances Wilson was appointed "his duenna" with a salary of twenty-two pounds a year "besides what is left of his rations." Later her wages were increased to thirty pounds, for to act as duenna to "an old lion" who has "the impulses of a tiger," throws his plate out of the window or dashes it on the ground if he dislikes his dinner, and suspects servants of opening desks, entailed, as Mrs. Browning observed, "certain risks, and I for one would rather not meet them." But to Wilson, who had known Mr. Barrett and the spirits, a few plates more or less flying out of the window or dashed upon the floor was a matter of little consequence—such risks were all in the day's work.

That day, so far as it is still visible to us, was certainly a strange one. Whether it began or not in some remote English village, it ended in Venice in the Palazzo Rezzonico. There at least she was still living in the year 1897, a widow, in the house of the little boy whom she had nursed and loved—Mr. Barrett Browning. A very strange day it had been, she may have thought, as she sat in the red Venetian sunset, an old woman, dreaming. Her friends, married to farm hands, still stumbled up the English lanes to fetch a pint of beer. And she had eloped with Miss Barrett to Italy; she had seen all kinds of queer things—revolutions, guardsmen, spirits; Mr. Landor throwing his plate out of the window. Then Mrs. Browning had died—there can have been no lack of thoughts in Wilson's old head as she sat at the window of the Palazzo Rezzonico in the evening. But nothing can be more vain than to pretend that we can guess what they were, for she was typical of the great army of her kind—the inscrutable, the all-but-silent, the all-but-invisible servant maids of history. "A more honest, true and affectionate heart than Wilson's cannot be found"—her mistress's words may serve her for epitaph.

P. 141. "he was scourged by fleas." It appears that Italy was famous for its fleas in the middle of the nineteenth century. Indeed, they served to break down conventions that were otherwise insurmountable. For example, when Nathaniel Hawthorne went to tea with Miss Bremer in Rome (1858), "we spoke of fleas—insects that, in Rome, come home to everybody's business and bosom, and are so common and inevitable, that no delicacy is felt about alluding to the sufferings they inflict. Poor little Miss Bremer was tormented with one while turning out our tea. . . ."

P. 147. "Nero had leapt from a top window." Nero (*c.* 1849-60) was, according to Carlyle, "A little Cuban (Maltese? and otherwise mongrel) shock, mostly white—a most affectionate, lively little dog, otherwise of small merit, and little or no training." Material for a life of him abounds, but this is not the occasion to make use of it. It is enough to say that he was stolen; that he brought Carlyle a cheque to buy a horse with tied round his neck; that "twice or thrice I flung him into the sea [at Aberdour], which he didn't at all like"; that in 1850 he sprang from the library window, and, clearing the area spikes, fell "plash" on to the pavement. "It was after breakfast," Mrs. Carlyle says, "and he had been standing at the open window, watching the birds. . . . Lying in my bed, I heard thro' the deal partition Elizabeth scream: Oh God! oh Nero! and rush downstairs like a strong wind out at the street door . . . then I sprang to meet her in my nightshift. . . . Mr. C. came down from his bedroom with his chin all over soap and asked, 'Has anything happened to Nero?'—'Oh, sir, he *must* have broken all his legs, he leapt out at *your* window!'—'God

bless me!' said **Mr. C.** and returned to finish his
shaving." No bones were broken, however, and he
survived, to be run over by a butcher's cart, and to
die at last from the effects of the accident on 1st
February, 1860. He is buried at the top of the gar-
den at Cheyne Row under a small stone tablet.

Whether he wished to kill himself, or whether,
as Mrs. Carlyle insinuates, he was merely jumping
after birds, might be the occasion for an extremely
interesting treatise on canine psychology. Some hold
that Byron's dog went mad in sympathy with Byron;
others that Nero was driven to desperate melancholy by associating with Mr. Carlyle. The whole
question of dogs' relation to the spirit of the age,
whether it is possible to call one dog Elizabethan,
another Augustan, another Victorian, together with
the influence upon dogs of the poetry and philosophy
of their masters, deserves a fuller discussion than
can here be given it. For the present, Nero's motives
must remain obscure.

P. 160. "Sir Edward Bulwer-Lytton thought himself invisible." Mrs. Huth Jackson in *A Victorian
Childhood* says, "Lord Arthur Russell told me, many
years later, that when a small boy he was taken to
Knebworth by his mother. Next morning he was

in the big hall having breakfast when a strange-looking old gentleman in a shabby dressing-gown came in and walked slowly round the table staring at each of the guests in turn. He heard his mother's neighbour whisper to her, 'Do not take any notice, he thinks he is invisible.' It was Lord Lytton himself" (pp. 17-18).

P. 169. "he was now dead." It is certain that Flush died; but the date and manner of his death are unknown. The only reference consists in the statement that "Flush lived to a good old age and is buried in the vaults of Casa Guidi." Mrs. Browning was buried in the English Cemetery at Florence, Robert Browning in Westminster Abbey. Flush still lies, therefore, beneath the house in which, once upon a time, the Brownings lived.